VILEM TAUSKY
TELLS HIS STORY

A Two-part Setting

First published in Great Britain
by Stainer & Bell Ltd
82 High Road London N2

ISBN: 0 85249 478 5

Printed in Great Britain

VILEM TAUSKY TELLS HIS STORY

A Two-part Setting

Recounted by Margaret Tausky

STAINER AND BELL: LONDON

Contents

		page
Preface		7
Part one		
1	A boy is born	8
2	Music ho! Sound music!	15
3	A musician in the making	24
4	Leo Fall was my uncle	30
5	Ten years at Brno Opera House	37
6	The clouds gather	48
Part two		
7	A new start	67
8	A soldier makes music	74
9	The Carl Rosa	86
10	Freelance of necessity	101
11	Ten years with the BBC Concert Orchestra	118
12	Cakes and Ale freelance by choice	137
13	The return of the native	145
	Epilogue	157
	Appendix	159

For Vil
'What I have done is yours, what I have to do,
is yours; being part in all I have, devoted yours'.
(Shakespeare, dedication of *The Rape of Lucrece*)
Peggy

Preface

The other day the telephone rang and a voice enquired, 'Is Vilem Tausky there? It's a reporter from the *Evening Standard* speaking'.

I replied, as I have so many hundreds of times before and since, 'I'm sorry, he is not here at the moment. It's Mrs Tausky speaking, can I help you?'

'Oh, good', replied the voice, rather to my surprise, 'Ken Loveland of the *South Wales Argus* told me to speak to you if possible—you're supposed to know more about Vilem Tausky than he does himself.'

Of course it's simply not true. For much of the time I have no idea what goes on in that large, well-shaped head, let alone in the heart. But in another sense I suppose it *is* true, for Vilem is eternally preoccupied with the work he is going to do today, tomorrow and next week. He finds little time for the fashionable occupation of shaping his lifestyle, and certainly wouldn't have the patience to write about the form it has taken. From time to time he has been prepared to talk to me about his life, and only those who know me well will appreciate how thorough my investigations have been when Vilem was in the mood to tell. *He* doesn't find his story particularly romantic, but I did, and in the quarter of a century that I have been his wife, I have continued to do so. I would love other people to enjoy it with me, and this is why you must accept me as the narrator of this story in which a life has been as neatly bisected as was the apple on the head of William Tell's son.

PART ONE

1 A boy is born

So my wife finds my career romantic. I can't say that it feels like that to me. It seems more like a great deal of hard work, a few disappointments and some enormously rewarding times which have often arrived at the most unexpected moments. Only in one direction do I admit an element of romance. I really can say that I was born under a lucky star, because the musical tradition into which I was born had its roots in two streams of music dating back to the days before World War I.

On my mother's side of the family, Leo Fall, the composer of the well-known operettas *The Dollar Princess* and *Madame Pompadour*, was her cousin, and her brother, Leo Ascher, who wrote *The Princess* waltzes, also became a successful operetta composer in New York. I was lucky enough from the age of seven to meet Franz Lehar and Oscar Straus, to listen to their café conversations, to watch them at the card table, to be introduced to their publishers and to visit their homes. Those were the days when Bruno Walter might conduct *The Merry Widow* and *The Magic Flute* in the same week; when we agreed that, as Brahms said of Johann Strauss, 'It is more difficult to write a good waltz than a bad symphony'.

Anna Mahler herself told me how much her father enjoyed Uncle Leo Fall's music, and after the war she gave me all the Fall scores from his library, which I still use. She also told me how, after one particular first night which the Mahlers had attended, her father and mother had an argument about a certain waltz tune and how it was developed. The next morning they visited the publishers used by both Fall and Mahler and, while Alma discussed sales promotion, Gustav took a peep at the Fall score, returning it to his wife with a triumphant, 'Told you so!'.

You can imagine that, growing up in this atmosphere, I have little patience with the division of music into 'serious' and 'light'. In fact, I wage an eternal crusade against it. In later years I used the BBC Concert Orchestra as number one propaganda in this cause.

Sometimes today, when I am spoken of as 'an authority on Viennese music', and people ask for more and more concerts of this kind at the Albert Hall and in the provinces, I feel inclined to grumble, 'Haven't they had enough?'. But in my heart I know that I should feel privileged that I am able to carry on an unbroken tradition from these great musicians. After all, we need music to reflect every situation in life: music for gay occasions, for melancholic moods, and to make us laugh as well as cry. The only difference I recognize is that between good and bad music, and this hasn't necessarily anything to do with the mood or subject chosen by the composer.

As it happens, the early musical influences in my life were as important in symphonic and operatic music as they were in the sphere of light music. I owe loyalty not only to two streams of music, which I personally see as a unity, but also to two countries. To Czechoslovakia for giving me my musical inheritance and education, and to England for giving me the opportunity to put it to good use.

I arrived in this world in 1910 as an afterthought, or so I always felt, for, in a family of four children, I was the youngest, born five years after my brother and nine years after my elder sister. I think the early circumstances of my life had a strong influence on the kind of musician I have become.

My father was a doctor in the service of the State, looking after the health of the railway workers at Přerov, a small Moravian town, but important as a railway junction. He was also private practitioner to the town and the country people around it. He was greatly loved and respected and people from miles away would come to fetch him in their own horsedrawn vehicles in cases of illness. Sometimes I or one of the other children would go to keep him company. In the town he was a well-known figure, paying his daily visits on his bicycle. He was utterly absorbed in the practice of medicine. His work, his family life and music-making in the evenings were almost his only interests.

My mother was born in Vienna and was of a lively tempera-ment, physically exuberant, blue-eyed, with long, black, curly hair that she could sit on. While still a young girl, she was discovered to have a beautiful singing voice and began her training at the Vienna State Opera. I still have some of her scores with Mahler's markings in them, and in one place in Mozart's *Marriage of Figaro* he has marked the sheet so emphatically that the pencil has pierced the page.

My father delighted in telling the story—'A wonderful career lay ahead of your mother, but she had to choose and she chose me . . . she has never regretted it!'

Mama always cast down her eyes and offered no comment.

We were a happy family, moderately prosperous, enjoying music and books together, my mother's occasional outbreaks of temperament saving family life from becoming too insipid.

Of the four children I was most like my mother, both in temperament and appearance. As a young child my great aims in life were to gain as much of my mother's attention as possible and to keep up with my lively brother and sisters, all considerably older than I was.

I have been told that my mother spoiled her curly-headed, blue-eyed 'Benjamin', but all I remember is that I always wanted my own way. My passionate outbursts of temper when I failed to get it led to incarceration in the cellar or the cloakroom. I remember lying down and kicking the door so fiercely that no amount of fresh paint could cover the bootmarks. The rest of the family used to tease me about my temper, but Father was quite adamant. 'In all that concerns yourself alone you can do as you like, but in what concerns us all you must learn to conform.'

That was the rule of our household, and I suppose a very old-fashioned way of treating children by today's standards. But it stood me in good stead when I had to earn a living in music, and even more so when I had, as a musician, to spend seven years in the army.

By the time I was four years old World War I had broken out and we Austrians were on the losing side. My very first memory is of Grandfather arriving from Vienna in the autumn of 1914. He brought me a toy cannon which fired rubber bullets. I had seen such a cannon drawn by horses through the streets of Přerov and opposite our house was a livery stable where these horses were watered and fed. As I watched from the window, clutching my own toy cannon, I identified with what was happening across the road, feeling the satisfaction that I, too, was part of the exciting grown-up world in which everyone was talking about 'THE WAR'.

In 1915 my father was called upon to help with the transporting of wounded soldiers on the railway from the Russian front. My mother had somehow to feed a hungry household and food was becoming more and more difficult to find. Luckily, some of my father's patients in the country remembered his kindness in the past and often sent little presents of eggs, butter, fruit—whatever there was to spare. When I was about six years old, our piano teacher, Miss Flora Herz, who came to teach us each week, said that her father, who was a manager of a farm, had a little flour to spare if someone could fetch it. Mother thought that a small boy with a knapsack on his back would not be noticed, so I was packed off one morning at 4 am to travel on the train to fetch the flour. I was back in time for school at 8 o'clock, mission accomplished!

Because my father was an army doctor, the family was entitled to fetch a loaf of maize bread from the station every day. Nevertheless, a photograph taken at that time shows me looking thin, pale and obviously undernourished. At the end of the war I soon made up for lost time, and certainly have never looked undernourished since.

That was the year I started school and I found it very enjoyable in the early stages. I dearly loved my first teacher and tried very hard to please her, but later on it was a different story, as I found school hours an excellent opportunity for dreaming about music, and writing it too—under the desk!

During the second year of schooling, in common with all the other children, I changed my nationality. I had been born an Austrian and I became a Czech on 28 October 1918 when Dr Masaryk's vision of a Czechoslovakian Republic became a reality and three hundred years of Hapsburg rule came to an end. On that morning I remember looking out from the very window where I had clutched my toy cannon and watched the soldiers on their way to the Russian front. Now I was looking at the tobacconist's across the road, surmounted, as State-owned shops were, by the Austrian double eagle. As I watched I saw the laughing, cheering crowds tear down the symbol of oppression and pass on their way rejoicing.

In many ways our community was a very tolerant one. We were a Jewish family, but my sister went to a convent school, where my mother was friendly with the nuns, and sometimes sang in the mass. The Roman Catholic priest always came to our synagogue on the Day of Atonement, and Magda Šantruček, Antonín Dvořák's daughter, born a Catholic, organized her concerts on the Protestant premises of the Czech Brethren.

It was through her that, at the same time as I was learning about the world of operetta through my family background, I was also learning about a different kind of music through family friend-ships. Magda lived in our little town where her husband, Dr Šantruček, was head of the local hospital, and thus he had professional connections with my father. Her friendship with our family was very important to me. I loved to hear her talk of the European concert tours with Grieg, in which she sang her father's songs in the first half, followed by those of Grieg. She and my mother used to sing duets together, and she helped to arrange some of my earliest concerts.

Paní Anna Dvořáková, the composer's widow, used to come every year to visit her daughter. When I was about ten years old I was taken to meet her and this occasion made a deep impression on me. Although I was so young, I remember thinking, 'This is the woman who prepared his meals, who sat by his side through the years and saw the wonderful scores grow under his hand, who shared the moments of triumph with him!'

She was a very sweet, simple person, but perhaps she realized something of the very real awe that I felt, for, to my great joy, she gave me a corrected page from his opera *Jacobin*, the opera in which my sister happened to be singing at that time. Paní Dvořáková must have had many such pages in her possession, for Dvořák would never allow a corrected page to go into the score, declaring, 'What is clear in the head must be clear on the paper'.

It was about this time that I met Josef Suk too. He was Paní Dvořáková's son-in-law through his marriage to Otilka, another daughter long since dead. I was fascinated to hear her call him 'Pepiku', our diminutive for Josef, and I little dreamed that one day I would be his pupil.

Certainly this circle, in which Magda Šantruček was a singer, my mother an opera singer and my sister an élève at the opera house, first turned my interest in the direction of opera. For over half a century I have worked with great singers of every nationality, from Chaliapin to Owen Brannigan, from Margherita Grandi to Joan Hammond. As opera was my first love in the world of music, so it has remained my greatest love. Today I feel the most important work I can do is to pass on to young people the experience I have gained in a lifetime of work in opera houses. It is as director of opera at the Guildhall School that I have this opportunity.

Everyone in our family spoke and understood both Czech and German. My mother all her life was by temperament and language Viennese. She spoke Czech in the shops and to the maids, but never completely mastered the grammar. To us she spoke German. My father, of course, as a doctor needed perfect Czech for his patients, but at mealtimes we always used both languages. In school the teaching of Czech history, art, literature and music in the Czech language gave children a sense of identification with the new nation.

And now, if you are to understand the assets which were mine when my life split in two, and also the adjustments I had to face, I must explain the geographical situation in which we lived.

I am a true son of Moravia, for I was born on its most fertile plain, in the district of Haná. The land is flat and rich, and the people are mainly employed in agriculture. Dvořák wrote an opera called *Hard Heads* (Tverdé Palice); think of the plots of Smetana's operas, *The Bartered Bride*, *The Kiss* and *The Secret*! They were describing my people; their temperament is obstinate. So is mine, as anyone who has worked with me can testify.

Přerov, where I was born, had been a stronghold of the Moravian Brothers, who stood for Protestant determination against the Catholic Hapsburg dynasty. When I was old enough to begin the second stage of my musical education, I went to the nearest town, Olomouc, which was a seat of musical culture in Haydn's time and had its own opera house and concert hall. By the time I was seventeen I had gained a place at the Janáček Conservatoire at Brno.

It was within the triangle of these three towns that the musical education was laid on which I have drawn during the forty years that I have lived in England. My inheritance was a rich one. People say that every Czech is born with a fiddle under his pillow. Certainly the people among whom I grew up found their recreation and entertainment in folksong and dance. Smetana and Dvořák, by their use of national melodies and rhythms, had already helped to bring the attention of the world to the rich musical inheritance of the Czechs, and it was in this part of the country that Janáček made his great collection of two thousand folksongs.

I was fortunate to be born in a part of the country so rich in natural music, but luckier still to receive my training from musicians such as Janáček, Suk and Martinů who were building out of the natural material around them some of the most forward-looking music in Europe.

2 Music ho! Sound music!

Most musicians will tell you that they can't remember the time when music became an influence in their lives. Funnily enough, I can tell you exactly how it happened in my own case.

Musical evenings were the main social interest in our family life, and of course friends sometimes joined us to play or listen. My father had a friend, who was often with us, called Karl von Pauspertl, a pianist and composer who later became a very popular figure in Vienna; you might call him the Willy Boskowsky of those days. There was another friend, called Pfennikl, who worked with my father as a medical orderly on the railway, and who often joined us on these evenings with his violin. He played the first piece of music I ever remember loving. It was called 'The Hot Canary'. As the youngest member of the family you can imagine how hard I fought against going to bed on these evenings. So my mother and I struck a bargain. After supper, if Pfennikl would play 'The Hot Canary', I would go to bed, but the bedroom door had to be left ajar so that I could hear the music-making. I imagine I learned a good deal about the mood and shape of music in this way, for children relax and listen well when they are alone.

My great friend in the family was my sister, Vally, seven years older than I, and already taking music and singing lessons from Miss Flora Herz. Girls love to impart what they have learned to those younger than themselves, so what more natural than that Vally should begin to teach me musical notation? I seemed to pick this up quickly, and very soon it was suggested that I could be present at the music lessons; in no time at all I was having half an hour's lesson myself. This would have been during my fifth year.

In about a year's time I was able to play my mother's accompaniments, although I couldn't read a book. At this time the great family joke was for my mother to say, 'Bring me the Carmen, Viloušku!', or 'I'll sing the Tosca tonight'.

I would trot over to where the scores were kept, and look, not *outside* at the cover which I couldn't read, but *inside* at the notes which I could. And I never quite understood why they laughed!

When my mother sang at these informal evenings, my father, who was a good pianist, had always accompanied her. But now, by my seventh year, how thrilled I was sometimes to be allowed to do so. There was a rather grand, blue velvet suit which I wore on these occasions, and I don't know which was the prouder, I of the suit or my mother of the accompanist. I can't think my phrasing can have been very fluid, but the notes must have been fairly accurate or the family would have howled me off the piano stool.

In my seventh year began the romance of a lifetime, for in that year I heard my first opera. In Přerov we had a concert hall-cum-theatre, which was also used for opera. Every Monday evening the company from Olomouc brought either a play or an opera to Přerov, and when I was seven my sister took me to hear *Carmen*. There was no sleep for me that night, only a very overwrought state and nightmares. However, I was determined to hear more opera and the next time it was *Tosca* to which I went by myself. I was fascinated, but quite unperturbed, by Tosca's fate. Even now I can't understand why I was so much more distressed by Carmen's death. Possibly because I knew the Puccini music so much better through my mother's singing.

After that, every Monday night that I had a crown in my pocket found me waiting at least an hour before the performance for a standing place as near to the orchestra as possible. As there was no rail I usually managed to sandwich myself between two double basses and, consequently, my first reading of operatic scores was through that instrument.

My determination to be as closely integrated into the orchestra as possible led to one of my earliest contacts with a really great musician. I remember that, one Monday night, the Czech-born Oscar Nedbal, an international conductor and the composer of the famous operetta *Polenblut*, was directing Smetana's *Hubička* (The Kiss). He was a giant of a man, and at the end of the first act, as he left the rostrum, he trod with all his weight on my foot. I let out a yell and good-naturedly he stopped to enquire, 'Did I hurt you?' Seeing the tears on my cheeks, he said, 'Follow me'. In the green-room he gave me a piece of chocolate. 'What are you doing out so late?' he said, 'Do you come for the music or haven't you got a home?'

I walked home on air; it was ten times worth the painful foot to have been spoken to by the great man.

Another memorable evening for Přerov was that on which the great Emma Destinn sang in Smetana's *Dalibor*. It is a splendid opera for a boy to hear, with its heroic quality, but I only realized what a unique evening it was when my mother explained to me that Destinn was a world-famous singer who had returned to her homeland to teach at the Prague Conservatoire.

By the time I was seven, I was able to play the piano pretty well for my age. I think, however, I discern one difference between myself and other musical children I have known. Most young children seem to be interested primarily in melody, a few in composing tunes and some getting as far as an interest in being able to write them down. Now, from my earliest days, although I wanted to be able to play the notes that produced sounds I liked, I wanted even more to be able to write a score. I saw music as a picture and, when I looked at quartets, my chief aim was to write music that looked like that. I didn't care so much how it sounded. Write music freely I did by the time I was seven or eight, but naturally it didn't always make sense.

Brass bands have always been tremendously important in the life of the Czech people. In my case, perhaps, it was also a family inheritance, for my mother's uncle, Moritz Fall, father of Leo Fall, was a regimental conductor in the Austrian army at Olomouc. He had three sons whom he trained mercilessly in the writing, orchestrating and playing of music in general, and brass band music in particular. Perhaps some of that blood flowed in my veins. I loved brass bands, and in my old age I am returning to an interest in music for brass, because I see it as full of unexplored possibilities. Anyway, in Přerov all important events were accompanied by brass music: mass in church, civic events, the birthdays of local dignitaries and last, but not least, funerals. I must have seemed a morbid little boy, for whenever I heard of a funeral afoot there I was to be found, following the mourners at a respectful distance. On the way back from the cemetery it was the custom to play a spirited march to conduct us back to life, and to join in this return march was my sole purpose in visiting the cemetery.

When I was six my sister broke her ankle, and my father was accustomed, in the mornings, to adjust the bandaging, which was a painful process for her. One day as he was strapping it she cried out in pain, and, according to the family, I appeared in my nightshirt at the doorway, calling out, 'Don't die, don't die, you can't die yet! I haven't written the funeral march!'

Doubtless the influence of my cemetery visits was morbidly at work. But my sister and I had happier musical associations at about the same time. Every Sunday morning at 11 o'clock the local band played in our park, and that was my weekly treat. In fact any serious misdemeanour during the week was met by the threat, 'No band on Sunday for you!' My sister took me. We wore our best clothes and Vally would have loved to join in the fashion parade which strolled up and down the main path. But there was I, glued to the bandstand, watching every instrument, every gesture of the conductor, and the poor girl had to stay with me.

I must have been about ten when, one Sunday when I was glued as usual to the bandstand, the conductor turned round, handed me his baton and said, 'Come on, you carry on!' And I conducted . . . I conducted! I suppose he must have been tired of the sight of me standing around.

Nowadays, when at the Albert Hall I conduct the wonderful Strauss waltzes, the Radetzky March, the Tritsch-Tratsch Polka and all the other old favourites, people come to see me afterwards and are kind enough to say, 'But it's *so* Viennese, it's so authentic!' and most often of all, 'You make it look so easy', and I reply, with more than a grain of truth, 'Well, you see, I learned it in the park when I was six years old.'

I don't know exactly when, but not long after this Miss Flora Herz, my first piano teacher, disappears from the picture. Perhaps she got married, I don't remember, but at any rate she ceased to teach the Tausky children. Přerov had a fine church with a good organ and a tradition of notable organists, composers and choral music. In my day the Přerov organist, Beníšek, also acted as organist at our synagogue. By the time I was eight I started piano lessons with him. You may be sure that as soon as my legs were long enough he put me on the organ stool as well. After three years Beníšek felt that my musical education needed widening and he persuaded my parents that I should have lessons from Angela Drechsler in Olomouc. She was a very good teacher and, in a modest way, a composer herself.

My lessons were a two-hour session every Saturday afternoon. First came the Czerny or Beringer exercises and the scales, which I hated, but on which she insisted. Then the playing of a classical sonata or a Bach piece. The second part of the lesson, which I enjoyed much more, was a romantic or modern composition which I played and we then analysed. The end was the study of harmony, using Foerster, and counterpoint by Thuille. This part of the lesson I enjoyed best of all. Like most children I was not enthusiastic about practising.

Many years later dusk was falling as I was walking through the main Town Hall Square in Olomouc. There, on the third floor, in a house which faced me, were just two lighted windows. It was the room where Angela Drechsler taught me week by week, and I couldn't help wondering if some other small boy was there, working away at acquiring the elements of music.

The 1919 changes in the Czech educational system had led to an improvement in provincial music schools, and there was a fine one in Olomouc. Miss Drechsler taught there, and when she thought I understood enough of harmony and counterpoint, and was sufficiently advanced in piano technique, she approached my mother who knew the director, Professor Heidegger, as she sometimes sang with his orchestra. Between them they arranged that I should attend the school to study piano, theory and composition.

The end of term finale was never to my taste, as we had to play in pupils' concerts. All the music was learnt by heart and I was in constant trouble because I always knew the piece before I had conquered the technical difficulties. On one occasion, I remember, I had to play Dohnanyi's C major Rhapsody and my fingers refused to follow what I knew quite well in my brain.

These journeys to Olomouc were my first taste of independence and as important in helping me grow up as a person as they were to my musical development. On Saturdays I went to school in the morning, then raced home to fetch my music and my sandwiches for the 1.35 train to Olomouc—as the son of a railway doctor, I travelled free of charge. Like Dvořák, I have always been fascinated by railway travel and you cannot imagine the sense of power and freedom this journey gave me. The lesson over, there was the dash to the station to see if I could catch the express to Přerov instead of the slow local. In later years I often stayed on in the town and my father would join me, for you could hear really good concerts in Olomouc. I remember hearing the Vienna Philharmonic conducted by Franz Schalk, also the pianist Eugen d'Albert, the last living pupil of Liszt, and Jan Kubelik, the famous violinist.

Under Miss Drechsler and Professor Heidegger I was gaining a well disciplined musical education. This was not irksome to me, for at home I supplemented the dry bones of musical technique with fantasy dreams of operatic conducting. But I never really deviated from the determination to become a composer. The occasional dreams of conducting were mere flights of fancy, much as a boy, who has made up his mind to be an engine driver, may sometimes enjoy enacting the part of the guard of a train.

My earliest compositions were at the age of about seven and they were the result of looking at other people's scores and trying to make similar pictures of music. I was quite unselfconscious about this and my efforts were open for all to see. But at the time I began to work with Miss Drechsler, I took my compositions to her and she showed me where they wouldn't work and why. This led to selfconsciousness at home, and there was a lot of tearing up and burning of my earlier work because I felt it was childish and worthless. From that time on, for several years, all my work was hidden from the family, even to the extent that I bought my own manuscript paper. In fact it was believed in the family that I had lost my interest in composing. However, as I say, I was not too shy to show what I had written to Miss Dreschsler, and she helped me to continue to develop in composition.

One source of inspiration was the work of a very gifted cousin of mine called Otto who died of diphtheria at the age of thirteen. His father was a Kaiser's counsellor and, at the outbreak of the 1914 war, they were on holiday and were recalled to Vienna. Otto had contracted the fever and he died on the journey home. He had written poems, stories and dramas from a very early age, and after his death his parents sent to his close relatives a volume of his work called 'Unser Otto'. In this book I found a libretto called 'For one love' and decided to set it to music. What is more, I actually finished it. I think I had some dim idea that I would perpetuate his name.

After a time my compositions came to light again. It had been my wish for some time to write a sonata for my brother Karel, who played the cello. One Sunday, Siegfried Fall, a professor at the Berlin Academy, and Leo's brother, was visiting us with a cousin, Charles Handler, who was a cellist and, I may say, a better one than my brother. Charles said to me, 'Haven't you written anything for the cello?' I admitted that I had, and off we went to the music room next door to try it out. Siegfried followed us and apparently liked what he heard. He offered to help me to correct it and, two years later, it was this work, in a revised form, which gained me entry to the Brno Conservatoire.

During this time my reputation at school was growing steadily worse, for I thought about music all the time and was too lazy to do my homework. I was then occupied in writing and conducting a revue about Přerov with local amateurs and I also spent endless time and thought on preparing and conducting a school performance of *The Bartered Bride*.

Because of these occupations I was by now in serious danger of having to repeat a year's work at school. Of course, if I had failed to matriculate I should never have qualified to go to the university at Brno, but I was at that age when one's head is far too much in the clouds to realize the importance of school exams. But then something happened which pulled me up short, both as a musician and a scholar.

My brother and I were the best of friends and, where plants and animals were concerned, I shared his interests. I was always ready to help him on botanical expeditions, or in training Arco, our German sheepdog. For some time we had a pet tortoise in the garden, and when it died one day, my brother decided that, with the aid of a spirit stove, we should boil down the carcass until we obtained the animal's skeleton. It was a bright sunny day and, as I could see no flame, it seemed to me that the stove needed more methylated spirit. Carelessly I tipped on some more fuel and in a second I was on fire. With great presence of mind my brother clutched me to him and rolled us both in the damp grass, but not before I was so badly burned on the arms and chest that I bear the marks to this day.

My mother at once applied goose fat to the burns, which was the accepted treatment for those days, and my father administered laudanum on lumps of sugar. But I only called out again and again, 'Ice cream, ice cream!' which they gave me, and 'Dr Šantrůček!' whom I wanted, and him alone, to do the bandaging, although why being Dvořák's son-in-law should make him a better doctor, I don't know. Anyhow, he came and bandaged me and gave me a morphia injection after which I slept for nearly two days.

It was fully two months before I could play the piano or go to school again, and I have always felt that this hiatus, both at school and in my musical career, marked a turning point in my life. My mother gave me a little kitten to keep me company and my sister helped me to catch up with my neglected schoolwork, but I suppose I had many hours of forced inactivity in which to think things over. When I returned to school, from that time onward, I did just enough work to get by. As far as my music was concerned, a new period of intensive composition began under Professor Heidegger and Miss Drechsler, but, owing to the demands of my general education, I could still only be a Saturday pupil at the Olomouc School of Music.

3 A musician in the making

In the year 1927 I matriculated just before my seventeenth birthday, and this meant that I was eligible for a free place at Brno University. Now began the struggle with the family. My parents were quite willing for me to continue musical studies, but they wanted me to read for a degree in law at the university, as they thought that to depend on music as a means of earning a living was a risky business. I eventually appeared to agree, and applied for a place as a law student. At the same time, however, I submitted my cello sonata to the Janáček Conservatoire, asking for a place in the composition class. This I obtained and, as I had matriculated, I did not have to continue with general subjects and so could find the time for the necessary law studies.

In Britain I think it would be very difficult to achieve this, because most people become resident in a college, and both their intellectual and social lives are controlled to a certain extent by the discipline of the college. The authorities keep themselves informed on attendance at lectures and behaviour out of lecture hours, and each undergraduate has a tutor who guides his reading, and sets the subjects for his essays.

Law studies in a Czech university are differently structured. The attendance at lectures is not obligatory as the professors have their published text books, which supplement the lectures. The examinations are under state control, and have to be passed within a certain time of entering the university. The university is not closely concerned with other aspects of a student's life, and one might say that the only concern shown is for academic standards. This narrowing of loyalties gave me a much easier chance of keeping up with the work needed for two degrees than would have been the case if I had been studying in England.

At this time my sister, Vally, was an élève at the opera house and she and I shared digs in Brno, but by common consent we soft-pedalled the fact that I was studying at the conservatoire as well as reading law at the university.

I was so proud to become one of Janáček's students, and very sad when he died only eight months after I entered the conservatoire, yet so strong was his influence on those who worked for and with him that, throughout the four years I was there, the whole institution was permeated with his presence and his beliefs. Although he had so many revolutionary ideas, he believed that a sound traditional base must precede progressive ideas in the training of musicians. 'First you must know the rules,' he used to say, 'then sometimes you can afford to discard them.'

During the first few months I worked at the conservatoire I was very conscious of his presence, for he was often to be seen enjoying the sun on his bench in the garden and, whenever the mood took him, he would stroll over to the conservatoire to see what was going on, for up to the end of his life he took a personal interest in the students and their progress.

It was quite alarming to encounter him until one got used to his personality, although he himself would have laughed at the idea that there was anything to be afraid of. Imagine a stocky, rather tubby figure, full of energy, surmounted by an abnormally big head of bushy hair, and blazing blue eyes which lent force to all he said.

His speech was very characteristic and most alarming, for his words came out in a staccato stream, like a cross between a typewriter and a machine-gun. He often gave his operatic characters speech rhythms typical of his own way of talking, as in *Kat̆a Kabanová*, where the matriarch says, 'You have to learn better manners . . . better manners . . . better manners,' and this comment is repeated by instruments in the orchestra as well as vocally. All his life he spoke in a Moravian dialect; all his life he drew the material for his work from the people he lived among. This is how he felt about folksong: 'I have lived in it since childhood, in folksong the entire man is enshrined, his body and his soul, his milieu—everything. He who is rooted in folksong becomes a complete man!'

From this it is easy to see how, as a teacher, he was never distracted from the building-up of music in the place he loved best. He came to Brno as a choirboy and, with the exception of a year in Leipzig and Vienna, he lived his whole life there. To put Brno and Moravia on the musical map of Europe seemed to him a worthwhile task. He was a real father to his pupils, and took the most personal interest in their circumstances and progress. He was sometimes impatient with the less gifted and unadventurous students: 'What's in your head, boy, straw?'

I remember Chlubna, a favourite disciple of Janáček, telling us how on Sundays Janáček used to walk with some of his pupils to Moravian festivals in outlying villages, talking of music all the way. The exhausted students used to be glad to climb on a bus for the return journey, but not so Janáček who looked forward to the walk back.

I said at the beginning that he was a simple man—I meant simple in that he found wonder and enjoyment in the material of life around him—in nature, in animals, and in the everyday life of ordinary people. Out of his observation of these matters he built his philosophy of life. He studied natural sounds, perhaps more profoundly than any musician before him. His music embodies not only these sounds, but through them his comments and reflections on the meaning of life. Often I would see him sitting in his garden in the spring of 1928, the year he died. He loved flowers, as he loved animals. Cowslips, snowdrops, violets in particular gave him great pleasure. The birds he loved too, and would follow with delight how the nesting was going on in his garden. Blackbirds were perhaps his special delight. He was filled with the joy of God's creation and as a musician it came naturally to him to make notes of the sounds they made and the variation on these sounds. His interest in such rhythms extended to human beings as well. Out of his acute ear for the sounds the human voice actually *did* make in various situations, he made his most original contribution to the form of opera.

Instead of expressing emotion through melodic lines, he conveyed it through the actual sounds he had heard the human voice make in a similar situation. He noted not only the intonation and rhythm of the words, but the register in which the notes lay. When he wrote a part for a dog as an alto voice (in *The Cunning Little Vixen*), you may be sure that a baritone won't do. The fox, which he wrote as a soprano, cannot satisfactorily be sung by a tenor. In some productions this has not been understood.

The case of one little girl, who was the daughter of a game-keeper in his native village, shows how deeply he studied in order to achieve this revolution in operatic speech. He kept records of her speech patterns from infancy to womanhood. I have already mentioned how devoted he was to the life around him, so it is no surprise to hear that many of the characters in his operas speak with the rough speech patterns of the Lachian peasants on the borders of Moravia. But perhaps most often of all, they echo the staccato barking notes of his own voice.

He told students how he constantly listened to the speech of people going about their everyday lives, noting their intonations. 'I don't need to understand the words,' he said, 'I can tell by the tempo and modulation of speech how a man feels: if he is excited, if he lies, or if this is just a conventional conversation. I have been collecting these speech rhythms for over fifty years, and I have an immense dictionary. These are my windows into the soul of man, and when I need to find a dramatic expression I have recourse to my library.'

I cannot emphasize too strongly that in this way Janáček was the father of the transcendent idea in modern opera—speech realism. Perhaps the closest comparable idea is in Berg's *Wozzeck*, but there are few operatic composers today who do not show traces of this influence in their work. In connection with this, I must tell a good story against myself. I went to congratulate Britten on his great success in the *Rape of Lucretia* after the first night, and we started talking about *Peter Grimes*. I said to Britten, 'One can hear how strongly you were influenced by Janáček, and how cleverly you adapted his principles to the English idiom.'

To which Ben replied, 'Believe it or not, when I wrote *Peter Grimes* I had never heard a Janáček opera.'

Nevertheless, these were the new ideas in opera which were in the air from the beginning of this century, and Janáček was their earliest and strongest propagator. He transmitted them to the great musicians who taught us at Brno as students and were responsible for passing on his teachings to the whole world. I have mentioned Osvald Chlubna before. He was perhaps the musician closest to Janáček and was my teacher in instrumentation. One of the greatest advantages of his teaching was that we had the chance to listen to our own orchestration played by the students' orchestra, followed by a critical analysis. I remember, when I had to orchestrate the first movement of Beethoven's second piano sonata, how surprised I was when I heard it played. Naturally we did a lot of analyses of the orchestration of works by Dvořák and Janáček. We also worked with the Berlioz-Strauss Treatise on Orchestration which was given to me as a present from the Fall family. The exercise for my final was Debussy's *Reflets dans l'eau*, for such a big orchestra that I had to wait a long time to hear it played.

Our composition classes with Vilem Petrželka, another of Janáček's pupils, started very strictly. For the first term we did only compositions based on counterpoint for different instruments, such as fugues for piano or solo violin, or a double fugue for string quartet. My first serious work of this type was a prelude and fugue for organ. We were not allowed at this stage to become very romantic. Then came variations, pieces in sonata form and songs. A choice of subject was only permitted in the second year. My final composition for the degree was a sinfonietta for orchestra, which gained me also a place in the Meisterschule in Prague, to study under Josef Suk.

Zdeněk Chalabala, who was chief conductor at the opera house, was in charge of the conductor's class. By an excellent arrangement, each of the three pupils was able to have one hour a week with the students' orchestra. I remember my first effort which was the first movement of Beethoven's Pastoral Symphony. All went swimmingly until I came to the end, when I realized I didn't know with what gesture I should cut off the last bar.

The years between 1927 and 1931 were filled with hard work, for not only was I busy trying to acquire the general musical education that every professional musician needs, but my parents were happily under the impression that my energies were being devoted to studying for a degree in law. I had to devote a certain amount of time to this project as well and this is where the two-part setting becomes obvious for the first time.

4 Leo Fall was my uncle

In the last chapter I gave you a detailed account of the very privileged opportunities I was given to become a musician in what people are pleased to call 'serious music'. But the title of my story is 'Two-part Setting' and I want now to tell you about some other musical influences which were at work in my life from very early days and which I consider added another dimension to my skill as a musician. They were to help me throughout my career.

Leo Fall was my uncle and what a privilege that was! He was a hero figure to inspire any boy with musical ambitions. From a child, Uncle Leo's connection with my family helped me to absorb the spirit of Viennese music, Viennese life and the gaiety and frivolity of the world of those wonderful operettas. For make no mistake about it, the operettas really were a reflection of Vienna at the turn of the century. Opera cloaks *were* lined with scarlet; monocles *were* worn; champagne *did* flow and '*chambres séparées*' were in constant demand.

And Uncle Leo lived this way, as well as writing about it. He came from a family of musicians in Olomouc. His father was a regimental conductor in the Austrian army and Leo, from his early days, must have had social aspirations as well as a great gift for melody. He joined the army where the disciplined life and elegant uniform gave him the entrée he needed. You can see how his temperament and talent set him on the road which led to Vienna.

Uncle Leo was an excellent violinist and, in their youth, the two great Viennese operetta composers, Franz Lehar and Leo

Fall, sat at the same desk in the opera house orchestra. When Uncle Leo's father retired from the army, he founded a salon orchestra in Berlin and employed his three sons, who were all musicians, to do all his copying and arranging as well as playing in the orchestra. Here Leo doubtless laid the foundations of his gift for composition, for musicians may be born, but they also have to be made, and it is the bread and butter work that provides the experience of *how* to set down those inspired tunes.

Fall developed a gift for writing chansons for cabaret, and his melodies became the rage of Berlin nightlife. They were a welcome source of income, but he was afraid they might hinder his chances of writing serious music. He wrote two operas which were moderately successful, but from operetta circles came the offer of the libretto of the *The Rebel*. The first performance was a disaster, but there was one man present who rose to his feet and shouted, 'You are listening with your ears blocked. Bravo, Leo Fall!'

This supporter was none other than Victor Léon, who had just had an enormous success as the librettist of *The Merry Widow*. Léon offered his next libretto to Fall, and backed up his support by financing the show with his own money. The result was *The Merry Peasant*, first produced in Mannheim in 1907: it was a resounding success, the first of many for Leo Fall. It was performed in London two years later, with Courtice Pounds in the lead. Significantly, this operetta left behind the familiar world of counts and duchesses, champagne and intrigue, for a more robust setting in a story of country life. It was as brave a step as Bizet had taken before him, when he began his great opera, *Carmen*, with workers coming out of a tobacco factory, or when Britten defeated his critics with *Albert Herring*, although they had said, 'A greengrocer's shop is no venue for romantic music.'

Only three months after the production of *The Merry Peasant* came Fall's first great international success. I wonder how many people who have enjoyed Cole Porter's *Kiss Me, Kate*, knowing the story is adapted from *The Taming of the Shrew*, realize that this same plot was also used in 1907 for the operetta *The Dollar Princess*, this time with a New York setting and music by

Leo Fall. It was such an outstanding triumph that it was subsequently produced in capital cities as far apart as New York and St Petersburg. Its London première was at Daly's Theatre in 1909, with Lily Elsie in the title role. Fall showed in *The Dollar Princess* and *The Merry Peasant* that his musical genius was equally at home in a variety of settings. He could be robust or elegant, sophisticated or rustic, witty or sentimental.

By now Uncle Leo was a rich, famous composer, and we come to the first impact he made on me personally. Imagine me, aged about seven, on holiday with my family in Bad Ischl; there is a family gathering in the café. My coffee and cream cake are long since finished when in strides the magnificent figure of Uncle Leo himself, and if the astrakhan collar, the monocle and the cigar were not actually there, certainly they are felt to be there. 'Ham and eggs,' raps out the magnificent figure, and I am lost in admiration—not only is he a famous composer, but has the power to command ham and eggs; both these must be mine!

Now I am a little older—twelve years old in fact. It is the first night of *Madame Pompadour* in Vienna and Uncle Leo has not forgotten his family, he has made a box available to them. You can imagine how exciting an occasion this was to a boy who already had his own musical ambitions. As we were waiting for the curtain to rise, my mother and father pointed out among the glittering audience many notable musicians and singers. Then the lights were lowered, the curtain rose and, as I looked down on the shining head of the conductor, the famous head of Uncle Leo himself, I resolved, 'That's the job for me, that's what I want to do'—and so, in due course, I did!

When I was in Olomouc, many years later, walking along the main street, I saw a bus stop with the name Holešov on it. What memories came flooding back! For the Fall family lived in Holešov, and throughout my childhood there were regular visits between our family and theirs, notably when Uncle Siegfried, who was a professor at the Berlin Academy, Uncle Richard who was well known for his popular songs, or Uncle Leo, himself, were visiting their sisters. It was an attractive and hospitable house with a little stream in the garden where I loved to play as a child. Although I did not realize it in earlier days, the whole family provided a stimulating atmosphere. Hedwig and her invalid sister ran this household and Hedwig's husband, although not a musician himself, was interested in all music and gladly suffered the constant visits of the family musicians. Two other brothers were Karl, who was a painter, and Ernst, a journalist and writer. In this house interest in the arts was paramount, and music of all kinds was performed and talked about from morning till night.

In the earliest days I just enjoyed all this constant talk of music in the Fall home, as well as the splendid refreshments provided by the sisters, who were both good cooks. Gradually I struck up a particular friendship with Hedwig, who was an excellent pianist, and we used to play piano duets varying from Haydn to Bruckner and Mahler. When I was about ten years old, I started to visit Holešov on my own bicycle, every Sunday afternoon. Hedwig and I used to play our duets, then followed a sumptuous tea, and afterwards often a game of cards or, if Siegfried was on a visit, he would help me with my composition. Today I greatly value this involvement with the Fall family, who not only thought and talked about music, but who were accustomed to regard it also as a means of earning a living. Much newly-published music arrived regularly at the house, to be both artistically criticised and professionally assessed. I remember very well the excitement when the new edition of *Der Rosenkavalier* arrived.

I believe that before I had achieved very much in the field of composition, or of programme selection, I had learned a most important lesson for the professional musician, that he must be aware of what the music publisher or the public is likely to find acceptable. At the Falls' one constantly heard casual remarks like, 'It would balance the piece better if he had given the comic pair a stronger duet in the first half,' or, 'He certainly had a winner in the first eight bars of the main tune, but he should have persevered until he found a better follow on,' or, 'What good judgment Léhar shows in *The Merry Widow*, merely to suggest that wonderful waltz in the first act and only fully develop it in the third'.

These kind of comments were all part of the daily conversation in the Fall household, and unconsciously I learned to look at music from this point of view. I am not suggesting that it is the only, or the most important, consideration for the composer, but if he can, at an early stage, absorb it as one of the factors to be held in mind, it should not hinder his creative powers and may save him much disappointment. It is one of the disciplines in art that one learns to accept.

One saying of Leo Fall from this period I have always remembered was the test he had applied to his own wonderful waltzes: 'A melody which is to be retained by the public must be able to be played with one finger on the piano," he said. As examples he quoted the 'Blue Danube', 'The Skaters' Waltz', and 'Gold and Silver'. I have described how the first period of Fall's creative powers culminated in the great success of *The Dollar Princess* which brought him international fame. There followed a string of successful operettas from which he created a curious superstition: he believed that for him only a six-syllabled title (in German) would succeed and, funnily enough, on the only occasion that he allowed himself to be dissuaded from this rule, the result was a failure—*Der Nachtschnellzug* (The Night Express). In 1908 he wrote *Die Geschiedene Frau* (The Girl on the Train) and this was produced in London two years later, starring Phyllis Dare. The following year his curtain-raiser, *Brüderlein fein* (Darby and Joan), was first produced in the cellar of the cabaret of the Theater an der Wien and was later performed as a curtain-raiser in the Vienna Opera House.

Fall introduced some of the music of the earlier failure, *Der Rebel* (The Rebel), in a new piece, *Der liebe Augustin* (Princess Caprice), and this time it was a worldwide success. It was produced in London in 1912 with Cicely Courtneidge, Courtice Pounds and Harry Welchman in the cast. Four year later, in 1916, Fall's success was such that *The Rose of Stamboul* was the most performed operetta in Vienna after *The Merry Widow*.

By this date Leo was somewhat sated with success and turned his back on operetta. His great ambition had always been to write a comic opera for the Vienna Opera House and now he could afford the time to do this. He devoted four years to the writing of *The Golden Bird*, When it was performed in 1920 in Dresden, with Elisabeth Rethberg and Richard Tauber, sadly it met with only moderate success.

He decided to return to operetta, the sphere of music where his greatest talent lay. The years 1920–23 were his last period of creativity, and he finished his life with three great masterpieces, *The Spanish Nightingale*, written for the great Fritzi Massary, appeared in 1921; it was the story of Carmen and was a forerunner of *Carmen Jones*. In 1922 he followed this with *Madame Pompadour*, first produced in England in 1933, starring Evelyn Laye and Derek Oldham. In my opinion it is the highlight of all Leo Fall's operettas. It is still played on the Continent and I would very much like to see an English revival. *The Merry Cavalier* was his last complete work, finished and produced in 1923.

I must tell one more personal story of Leo Fall which, even after all these years, brings his personality, his generosity and his sense of fun vividly before me. Our family was fond of informal musical evenings, and it was our custom to enjoy 'eine kleine Nachtmusik'. Uncle Leo knew that my brother very much wanted a violin so that he could play in this group. One summer night, as we sat at dinner in the garden, the nearby hall was filled with magical music, played on the violin. Nobody knew that Uncle Leo was even in town, but this was his charming and highly individual way of presenting my brother with the fiddle he longed for.

Some wonderful musical opportunities came to us all through this family connection. On one occasion, as a young music student staying with Siegfried Fall in Berlin, I went with him and his great friend, Franz Schreker, the composer, to hear the young Menuhin, then aged fourteen, in a concert with the Berlin Philharmonic. He played the Bach E Major, then the Beethoven. After this, in the interval, my uncle said, 'Don't you think we should leave now, after two such magnificent performances we shall only be disappointed?' But Schreker and I were for staying, and that boy of fourteen gave an equally stunning performance of the Brahms: three concertos!

Years later in London I asked Menuhin if I was right in thinking that the conductor was Bruno Walter. 'I don't know,' he said, 'I gave that concert quite a few times.'

In the spring of 1925, Fall undertook a tour of South America and, although he was still at the height of his career, the strain of foreign travel, combined with personal problems, led to a physical breakdown. He returned to Vienna where he died in September of the same year at the early age of fifty-two.

He left so much musical material behind him that two complete operettas were arranged and published posthumously by Erich Korngold. Fortunately, he was unaware of the seriousness of his condition in the last months of his life. As he lay dying, he spoke these words to his wife—surely among the happiest a composer can utter—'Bertl, I have still so much to write'.

Leo's death was a tremendous blow to the Fall family. My connection with them continued for as long as I remained in Czechoslovakia. Siegfried had hoped that I would go to Berlin to study under his friend, Franz Schreker, but the rise of Hitler put an end to any such plan. Siegfried himself returned from Berlin in 1933 to live with his sisters in Holešov. During the course of the war the whole family was sent to the ghetto at Terezín, and now my only contact is with Leo's daughter, Rischka, who lives in Sweden.

I began this chapter by paying tribute to all that I learned in the Fall household, and indeed so much of it has helped me throughout my career as a musician. It has been of special importance in two particular phases of my life, one in each part of my 'two-part setting'. The first time was between 1933 and 1939, when my own operettas were being written and produced in Czechoslovakia. I was also then writing operetta in collaboration with Weinberger and Friml. The second time was in England, when, after I left the BBC Concert Orchestra in 1966, I found myself, to my own surprise, a conductor who specialized in Viennese music. This development was in no way sought by me and is a further proof of my theory that I have not made my career, it has been made for me.

5 Ten years at Brno Opera House

This chapter tells how the smell of greasepaint first filled my nostrils, from which moment Tausky the composer of the future became Tausky the conductor, and man of the theatre. There had always been the closest connection between the conservatoire and the opera house in Brno, because the principal players in the opera orchestra and the chief conductor were also teachers at the conservatoire and were always in touch with the potential talent among the students.

In my second year at the conservatoire, Fibich's opera *Šárka* was in rehearsal at the opera house, to be conducted by Chalabala. It so happened that his assistant, the repetiteur, fell ill and, on the strength of the work we had done on *Šárka* in class, he thought I would be the most suitable substitute to play for the production rehearsals. Afterwards he said to me casually, 'They liked you, you can come again'. So the die was cast, and during the next year I was used more and more in the theatre, while continuing my studies at the conservatoire. Eventually came the day when Chalabala told me to see the director, Jiřikovský, who offered me the post of repetiteur at the theatre, although I still had to finish my studies.

In about a year's time I had my first chance to conduct at the opera house. I had been working with Chalabala on *Turandot*, and when he fell ill himself I was offered the chance to take his place. It was quite a tricky job, for I was only told at eleven o'clock on the morning of the performance and we had two guest stars, each singing in his or her own language. I had one advantage however: having helped at the rehearsals I knew in advance what mistakes the other singers were likely to make. The two guests were Zinka Milanov (then Zinka Kuncová) singing Turandot in Croatian, and Jan Kiepura as Kalaf in Italian; the rest of the cast sang in Czech. I am not going to say that my name was made in a night, but it all went off reasonably successfully.

Next, in 1932, I prepared Roussel's ballet *Le Festin d'araignée* and for the first time I took full conductor's responsibility for a new production. I don't propose to take you step by step through the ten years I spent at Brno Opera House, but the next thing that happened to me was so fantastic that I must go into it in some detail.

Our theatre was agog with excitement because Chaliapin was coming to sing *Boris Godunov* and *Faust*. As Chalabala was ill again, I was asked to deputize for him. This time, although naturally I was pleased and excited, I really did quake in my shoes, and of course my colleagues were only too ready to tell me how cruel he was to conductors. Apparently it was his habit when he didn't agree with the conductor's tempo to step forward in full view of the audience and beat out with his foot the tempo acceptable to him. They also said, 'He won't sing a note for you at the rehearsal, he'll only put you through your paces on the piano'.

Jiřikovský, who wanted to prevent any scenes in the theatre between the great man and a very young conductor, sent me to Chaliapin's hotel in Prague to glean what help I could before the performance. Tremblingly I approached his suite, but he couldn't have been nicer, not only did he mark arias for me, but he went through the whole opera in the most helpful way. When it came to the performance, he only corrected me with his foot once, which I thought was a triumph.

The producer, Branko Gavella, had a bad moment, though. At the morning rehearsal Chaliapin strode on to the stage and looked around. 'Where did you say the Kremlin gate was?' The producer indicated the right-hand side of the stage. Chaliapin drew a knife from his pocket, walked over to the opposite side, and slashed the canvas from top to bottom. 'The gate is *here!*' he said, and that was that.

It really was fantastic for me to be conducting *Boris* for

Chaliapin at the age of twenty-one. However, this is the way that opportunities come to young conductors, and very hard they have to work to be in a position to earn them. As repetiteurs, we played for rehearsals from nine until twelve each day, coached every afternoon from two until five, and if we were not conducting offstage chorus or playing the celeste in the evening performance, we were expected to be watching to see what we could learn from it. But it is exactly such a background of donkey work which in the end makes an experienced conductor. Naturally, when opportunities arise they will be given to those who show enthusiasm for what is happening in the theatre rather than to those who try to skip some of the routine.

I thought I was a pretty hard worker, but the following little story illustrates the standard expected of us by Milan Sachs, the musical director. After lunch one day, I sat reading my newspaper and drinking a coffee, enjoying the sunshine at an outside table at the Café Opera. When I returned to the theatre there was a message for me to go and see Sachs. 'Oh, good,' I thought, 'I am doing pretty well, probably he is going to offer me another opera to conduct.'

Sachs greeted me with a steely look. 'Did I see you at the café, drinking coffee and reading the newspaper? Can you afford the time? Have you no scores to study?' Whether he meant to take me down a peg or two I don't know, but it certainly had that effect.

My conducting was checked further for the moment, as Sachs decided I was rather a good pianist and I was put to play piano solos for the ballet in *Firebird*, *Petrushka* and Martinů's *Špaliček*. I also played in a performance of a new opera, a western called *The People of Poker Flat* which used a new invention, an electronic piano. This was the first step in my long and important association with the opera's composer, Jaromir Weinberger.

At this time I was also learning about human nature in the theatre, and how to deal with it, from a man with a great sense of humour, Václav Jiřikovský, our administrative director. One day I was in his office when Dr Leoš Firkušný (Ruda's brother), who was his secretary, appeared saying, 'Paní Žaludová is here to see you, in a filthy temper because her dates have been altered'.

Hastily I made to leave, but Jiřikovský said, 'Stay here, young man, you may learn something to your advantage'.

Reluctantly I sat down, and in stormed the prima donna, 'What is the meaning of this injustice? My dates were fixed two months ago, and I have made my arrangements accordingly. Who is this Russian woman that her convenience should be studied before mine?' On and on she went, Jiřikovský listened silently, but gradually his eye brightened, slowly he rose and walked towards her, 'Tell me,' he said, 'is that a new outfit you are wearing? I don't think I have seen you in it before, the colour is so becoming, and that hat! It's so right with the whole ensemble.'

'Do you really think so? I am so glad you like it, the hat was my own idea.'

The tantrums subsided, the dates were smoothly adjusted, and as the door closed on Paní Žaludová the director said to me with a wink, 'Let that be a lesson for life to you, young man!'

Just as I told you how in the years at Olomouc I laid the basis of my technical knowledge of music, so in these ten years at the opera house I built up the experience of general operatic repertoire on which I have been drawing ever since. Naturally we were specialists in Czech opera, every season included some Smetana, Dvořák or Janáček. Since then I have had the pleasure of introducing the English public to several of these for the first time. As a Slav nation we also had a big proportion of Russian operas among our productions. I conducted *Eugen Onegin* (with Jarmila Novotná) *The Czar's Bride* by Rimsky Korsakov, and also *The Snow Maiden*, and many more including *Boris Godunov*, of which I told you. In Italian opera I did all the standards by Puccini, as well as Verdi's *Il Trovatore* with Zinka Milanov as Leonora and *Rigoletto* with Chalabala's wife as Gilda. A delicate situation to have the musical director's wife as your prima donna!

But for this relatively short period a great deal of my time in the theatre was given to ballet. It would not have been my choice, but I had to co-operate with whatever way the directors of the opera house chose to use me. As it happened, the knowledge I gained in this way helped me to find my first chance to earn a living when I left Czechoslovakia. I recently received an article published in a Brno newspaper which began: 'In the history of Brno, which was published last year, there is a section devoted to artists who brought honour and fame to their town and to Czech art throughout the world—there are listed four names— Vitězslava Kaprálová, Rudolf Firkušný, Vilem Tausky and Vánia Psota.'

It so happens that in the short period of my life concerned mainly with music of the dance, Vánia Psota and I were very closely connected. To begin with he was also a native of Přerov, where his mother had a dancing school. He and I attended her classes, and I often partnered his sister when we were all about seven or eight years old. As far as I was concerned it was a short-lived experiment; dancing was not for me. But Vánia went from strength to strength, and by 1932 was a member of the Ballets Russes. He visited England with the company and there made a great reputation in character roles, in such ballets as *The Good Humoured Ladies, La Boutique Fantasque* and *The Three-Cornered Hat.* When the Company was reformed under Colonel de Basil, he was again a member and visited England in 1936.

At this time my future wife was quite a balletomane, and during the two visits of the Ballets Russes she conceived a tremendous admiration for the character-dancing of Psota. When she and I met in 1940 it was not long before we started to talk of ballet, and she told me what a gifted dancer she thought Psota was, little knowing that we had been brought up together and had worked in the theatre in Brno together for years. In 1937 he returned to Brno to become ballet master and choreographer of our theatre where my childhood partner, his sister Ljuba, was now a member of the corps de ballet. Vánia and I prepared Prokovieff's *Romeo and Juliet* together, and *Apollon Musagète* by Stravinsky, but probably our most outstanding work was the première of *Signorina Gioventú* in which he directed and danced the main role. The music is by Vitězslav Novák. Vánia brought us invaluable experience from his international work with the Diaghileff Ballet, and our company achieved a very good standard under his direction and I was sad to hear of his death in 1955. I learned, while there on a visit, that I still hold a tenuous connection with the ballet in Brno, for a member of the orchestra told me they still use my orchestration for *Les Sylphides*.

At about the same time that I was busy with the preparation of ballets, our theatre was honoured by a visit from Richard Strauss who came to conduct his *Der Rosenkavalier*. It was a great day for Brno and a memorable performance, but it was also long remembered for an incident during the dress rehearsal. Strauss was pleased to find the orchestra and cast well prepared, and as he grew more and more confident that it would be a satisfactory performance he called out to the leader from time to time, 'We don't need this,' and skipped a few pages. When it came to Ochs' waltz at the second act he called out to the bass who was singing the role, a chap called Pribytkov, a typical slow-witted Russian, 'Do you need this?'

Pribytkov came down to the footlights and said to the great maestro, in his ponderous Russian, 'If you don't need it, *I* don't need it.'

When this was translated to Strauss he roared with laughter, and after that no one could take the rest of the rehearsal very seriously. The reply became a catchword in the theatre and for a long time conductors would enquire of their singers, 'Do you need this?' and promptly would come the answer, 'If *you* don't need it, then *I* don't need it.'

On the tenth anniversary of Janáček's death, Brno Opera House performed the whole cycle of his operas, and of course this gave me an exceptional opportunity to study the operas, their production and the original scores. Probably the detailed information gained in this way caused Chalabala, who had conducted these performances, to choose me to help him on the final corrections of the score of *The Cunning Little Vixen*. Twenty years later the same score was sent to England and I recognised my own red-ink markings when I conducted from it in Manchester. The same happened with Dvořák's First Symphony, discovered in 1923, and first performed in Brno in 1934. Both these works, which I conducted, were given their first performance in this country by the BBC Northern Orchestra in Manchester.

I must explain that Janáček worked very differently from Dvořák who always taught his pupils, 'What is clear in the head must be clear on the paper,' whose own scores were immaculate and who would tear out a page rather than make a correction. Janáček was not at any time a tidy worker, and his operas needed considerable editing to become clear through the conductor or the performers. He also made changes up to the very last moment. When *The Macropoulos Case* was being produced, he attended the rehearsals and kept interrupting to make adjustments. Even at the final dress rehearsal he was still interposing with suggested alterations. At last the conductor lost his temper, 'This is impossible,' he shouted. 'No more changes!'

Janáček appeared to accept the situation and disappeared. But on the first night, at a certain point, the cello leader looked up at the conductor in astonishment; the conductor maintained his beat, but in equal bewilderment—both were hearing music they had never heard before. Although Janáček appeared to have been defeated, what he had done was to go to the library after the music was put away and write into the cello part a solo which he felt should be there.

Before his death in 1928 he left Brno to go on holiday, telling the theatre authorities he had finished the score of *From the House of the Dead*, although he took the score with him which was contrary to his custom. The opera should have been produced in the new year and, naturally, after his tragic and unexpected death, it was planned to honour him by securing a production as soon as possible. But before much progress could be made, Neumann, who had conducted all his first performances, died very suddenly. When those responsible came to study the score it was found that, although the opera was finished, it was far from ready for production. The orchestration had many incomplete passages, and some parts of the libretto were in Lachian dialect, some in Czech and others in Russian. It needed considerable editing, and I worked with Chlubna and the producer, Zítek, first on the score, and then as repetiteur.

One of the problems of the opera was its conclusion. Janáček had ended the opera with the freeing of Petrovitch and the eagle, the captive symbol owned by the prisoners. But the main body of the prisoners, after a short burst of rejoicing, were driven back into the house of the dead by their guards, to the sound of relentless, merciless music in which is heard the clanking of chains. Both Chlubna and Zítek felt that this ending was not in keeping with Janáček's attitude to life and art, and also that it was theatrically a disappointment for the audience. Zítek therefore suggested that Chlubna should write a final seventeen bars, from Janáček's material, and instead of the prisoners being driven back into the house of the dead, they should remain singing triumphantly of freedom. This was the version used for the first production in which I was involved, but I have always wondered whether the alternative ending was the right one.

My two-part setting was never to escape me for long and suddenly, in the middle of all my work at the opera house, when I was so deeply involved in the intepretation of Janáček and other modern Czech composers, my own fortunes took another turn. By this time I no longer made any pretence of becoming a lawyer, but I was still anxious to justify myself in the eyes of the family. Now, quite unexpectedly, came an opportunity to carry on the Fall tradition, to realize my boyhood dream of becoming a composer of operetta. You will remember that our theatre had put on an opera by Jaromir Weinberger, in which I played a new instrument, the electronic piano. Jiřikovský, our director, was very friendly with Weinberger, and wanted him to write an operetta for us. Jaromir admitted to having a good idea, but had neither the time nor the inclination to carry it out in detail, so Jiřikovský suggested that I should collaborate with him. The result was *Na Růžích Ustláno* (A Bed of Roses) which was a very great success, first produced in Brno in 1933, then in Prague the following year, and at last in Vienna in 1937.

I collaborated with Jaromir in two subsequent operettas. The second one was called *By the Way, How is Andula?*, surely a very modern title for 1934. The last one before his final visit to Holly-wood, *The Emperor Picks Cherries*, was a little love story about Napoleon before the battle of Austerlitz. I worked with Wein-berger over a period of five years and came to know him very well. In fact I was with him in his box at the première of *Schwanda the Bagpiper* in Vienna in 1933, conducted by Clemens Kraus.

It was immediately an enormous success with the audience, and derided by the critics. I well remember on that occasion the famous critic, Korngold, father of the composer, wrote of the wonderful reception by the audience, and added: 'After the performance one of the composers was present, and took a bow for all the others'—a bitter sneer at what he felt to be the derivative qualities of the work. But Weinberger surmounted all criticism with real Czech obstinacy and optimism. If his friends were pleased and his audiences happy he snapped his fingers at the critics in true Schwanda fashion.

This was his first opera and his outstanding success. In spite of the critics, it was played in the next few years in seventeen languages and a hundred and fifty opera houses. Of course there was some truth in what his detractors had to say, that the influences of Smetana and Dvořák, and of his teachers, Vitězslav Novák and Max Reger, were sometimes all too apparent. His harmonies and orchestration were sometimes too brilliant, too elaborate for the simple folk story he was illustrating. Nevertheless, he was a composer with a keen sense of theatre, exceptional melodic invention and first class craftsmanship. I have always felt myself that the outstanding success of *Schwanda* was due to the fact that he found a hero figure who in many respects reflected his own personality. Schwanda in Czech folklore is a gay rascal who is always able in his lighthearted way to get the better of the other fellow. Jaromir Weinberger was himself a true Schwanda and enjoyed to the full his ability to express these qualities in music.

I learned a tremendous amount through working with him, and now I was to play a rather Schwanda-like trick on him myself. Polách and Žalman, who wrote his operettas and were excellent librettists, became interested in my music, and we started to write our own operetta together. Not that Weinberger cared, for he already had more ideas and more work than he could cope with. Our first venture *Marcella* was based on a new idea, operetta for radio. It was very successful and this gave me the idea to write a large scale radio opera on a serious subject. Žalman provided the material for a libretto about Christopher Columbus and this opera, *Cristobal Colon* was broadcast on 12 April 1934 and was awarded the State radio prize. You can imagine that with such a subject it contained a good deal of sea music. The great joke was that at that time I had never actually seen or heard the sea. Some of the money I earned helped me, the next summer, to remedy this, for I was able to afford six weeks' holiday on a little island off the Yugoslavian coast.

Then came my greatest triumph in the world of operetta. I had always had a feeling, possibly unjustified, that the family still felt, "Yes he is doing quite well, but will it last, is he relying on a series of lucky ventures, has he really chosen wisely?' And so I began an operetta with Polách and Žalman called *There's Always a Funny Side*, which opened in Brno on 5 May 1934. It was very successful and was produced in Sofia and then in Prague, but the great triumph was when it was chosen for the New Year's Eve performance in Prague that year. This is always a very special occasion in mid-European opera houses, when extra sparkle and glamour is looked for, both in the piece which is chosen and the artists who play in it.

I remembered the first night of *Madame Pompadour*, when I had said to myself, 'I could do that,' and, like Uncle Leo, I saw to it that all the family of Falls and Tauskys was there in force to share my hour of triumph. Although I have enjoyed many exciting occasions in the theatre I have never been so conscious of a dream come true.

In the Brno Opera House I think my career reached its zenith in 1938 when I was entrusted with a new and outstanding production of Dvořák's, *Rusalka*. It is a fairy tale full of fantasy and imagination. The producer was Jaroslav Kvapil, who had written the libretto for Dvořák, and he made wonderful use of our very modern stage resources to create the mysterious atmosphere of the magical forest. During the rehearsals Kvapil told us many stories of the great man, mostly concerning his poetic simplicity. The one which always remains with me concerns the time when Kvapil, as a very inexperienced young man, first took his libretto to read to Dvořák. Rusalka is the familiar story of a water nymph who longs to be human to gain the love of a prince, and the story ends in tragedy for them both. Dvořák listened silently, absorbed as a child. At the end of the reading he asked, 'What happens next?' and Kvapil, who had not finished the third act, told him in his own words the rest of the story. Anxiously he awaited the great man's verdict, but there was utter silence until Dvořák murmured to himself, 'Poor prince, poor prince!' and Kvapil saw that his eyes were full of tears.

In 1937 I began to work with two formidable composing talents, the first Bohuslav Martinů, one of our foremost modern young Czech composers. More important for me was another friendship formed in that year when I also rehearsed and conducted the first performance of an opera by the great Russian composer, Nicolai Tcherepnin. It is no exaggeration to say that before long I was to owe my life and freedom to my association with Tcherepnin and his opera, *Vaňka*.

6 The clouds gather

The fact that I am Jewish has, up to this point, had little importance in my story, and throughout my youth I always lived in a climate of toleration that drew little attention to my race. In religion I have never been an Orthodox Jew. In Přerov people of different religions worked happily together for the welfare of all. I have already mentioned that for about three years my musical education was in the hands of the local organist of the Roman Catholic church, who also played in our synagogue. When I began to learn the organ with him, I was allowed free use of the church organ on which I could practise at any time. The priest was very friendly with the whole Jewish community and, indeed, on the Day of Atonement, always made a point of coming to the synagogue for part of the service. My elder sister attended the convent school just across the road from our house, my mother was on the happiest of terms with the nuns, and would sing for them on special occasions in their chapel. Magda Šantručková, Dvořák's daughter, became a member of the Evangelical Church of the Czech Brethren, although Dvořák himself was a devout Catholic, and there she arranged the concerts of which I have already spoken. She cared only to assemble the best musicians who could be found locally, and I don't think any of us bothered about who was Jewish, Roman Catholic or Protestant.

This was the atmosphere in which I grew up, but by 1938 even I, who was inclined to ignore what I did not want to acknowledge, was forced to become aware of the dangerous political situation which was approaching ever closer. From 1933 the position of the German Jews grew constantly worse, though, curiously, in Czechoslovakia at this time Jewry was divided into two factions. Firstly there were Jews with traditionally German affiliations and loyalties. (Hitler was driving a wedge into the country by the territorial claim he made on Sudetenland where he insisted that the people wanted German nationality and protection.) Secondly, there were the Czech Jews, whose Jewish origin was of secondary consideration to themselves and to others, and these were primarily Czech patriots. Among these I was to be counted, and it seemed unbelievable, in the early years of his rise to power, that Hitler could reach out and engulf and destroy our little corner of the world.

Life in the theatre was absorbing, colleagues were as friendly as ever, and, most exciting of all in the world of operetta, 'Beda' (Dr Fritz Löhner), the famous librettist of Léhar and Kalman, was offering me his book for an operetta which promised a première in Vienna. Was it surprising that I did not want to take action about the political situation? For there was really only one course open to me, namely to leave my country, my friends and my work. But after the Munich crisis it was impossible to ignore the way things were going. Gradually the Nazi influence was penetrating the ranks of the Czech nationals, as I clearly saw in the first incident which affected me personally. I had a contract to write the music for a film illustrating Czech national life. A letter arrived cancelling the contract on the grounds that I was not a suitable person to write music of this character. My lawyer advised me to challenge the cancellation and although the principal of the conservatoire gave evidence of my Czech education and patriotism, the case was decided against me, and I was ordered to pay costs.

Eventually the precariousness of my own situation was brought home to me in the most dramatic way. I had written an operetta called *The Girl in Blue*, first produced in Brno and followed by a production in České Budějovice, in South Bohemia, not far from the Austrian border. I was to conduct the first performance there.

All went well, it was enthusiastically received and I went to bed with my head full of a successful first night. I woke in the morning and looked out into the square below to see German tanks rolling by and swastikas hanging from the windows. Quickly I packed my things and made for the railway station, took a train to Brno and arrived only to find the same situation there. From that moment there was only one solution, to get out as quickly and unobtrusively as possible. It took me nearly a month, and during that time I experienced some of the most frightening moments of my life. I also learned what friendship can mean.

First, I went to my flat, where my Jewish landlady lived on the upper floor. She advised me to leave my permanent possessions there, but to find other accommodation where I could keep everything I was likely to take with me if I were able to make a getaway. 'I'm afraid if they come for us they might take you too,' she said, 'Go to Paní Růžičková, she will help you.'

Paní Růžičková was a friend of hers, an Aryan lady, and the mother of my girlfriend. She said at once, 'Of course you must stay with us, until you can arrange something'. This in spite of the fact that on the ground floor of the same house there was a Nazi café. Here was courage!

Next I went to see another Aryan, our director Jiřikovský. 'You must get out as soon as possible', he said, 'We'll see what we can do. You'll need money too. I might be able to arrange something there as well.' It so happened that Janáček's opera, *Jenufa*, was to have its première in Paris that season and Jiřikovský was sending his son, Václav, with the costumes which the Paris Opera was borrowing from Brno. His idea was that he should inform Paris that I was coming with Václav, and that once I got to Paris I could probably help with the preparations for *Jenufa*. It would also be a protection for me to travel across Europe in Aryan company. My main problem, however, was to obtain visas for leaving Czechoslovakia and for entering France.

You will remember that the Russian composer, Nicolai Tcherepnin, had entrusted me with the première of his opera, *Vaňka*, and he himself had attended this in Brno. I had in my possession a most grateful letter from him written from Paris after his return, saying that if he could ever help me in any way to be sure to let him know. It was a slender chance, but I sent this letter to my brother-in-law in Prague who took it on to the French Embassy, and on the strength of this letter, and the fact that the writer was the principal of the Russian Paris Conservatoire, I was granted a French visa. It was tremendous luck, but a harder task still remained—to obtain an exit visa from the Gestapo. Jiřikovský said, 'You will need two thousand crowns *We* need an orchestration for an operetta on Bizet's music. While you are waiting for your papers, make this orchestration for us. Leave the money with me, and I think the passport will be forthcoming.'

Quite how it was managed I never knew. To obtain the exit visa it was necessary to soften up a certain *Gauleiter*, and to this end there was a party given by three of our girls from the ballet for him and his friends. Within a few days I was told by Jiřikovský to call at the Gestapo headquarters at 10 am on the following Saturday. It was a terrifying prospect for a Jew even to attempt to pass the guards, and when that was safely accomplished there was still the ordeal of asking for my papers. Jiřikovský had assured me that all would be well, but there was always the chance that although the *Gauleiter* had swallowed the bait he would nevertheless refuse the visa, or even arrest me. With a beating heart, I asked for the official concerned. He produced my passport with the exit visa, scrutinized them and me, and handed them over. Then, with a twinkle in his eye, he wished me luck and shook hands. Directly I felt it was safe, I inspected the passport, and sure enough the fatal 'J' for *Jude* was not stamped on the front. Jiřikovský had saved me, as he saved so many others. I was so sad to learn later that during the war he was executed as a result of his liberal principles.

My mother had died in 1937, and we were all thankful that she had not had to suffer the break-up of her family. My father continued to practice medicine in Přerov, for he could not believe that the local people would ever turn against him, and indeed they never did. My elder sister and her daughter went to keep house for him until they were all ordered by the Gestapo to the Russian front—as far as we know, he as a doctor, and she as an assistant nurse. They were never heard of again, and I was unable to see my brother and younger sister, who had estates near the Hungarian border, for it was dangerous for Jews to travel. I managed to reach Přerov once or twice in the month during which I awaited my papers, but there was no definite leavetaking, as I had no idea when the necessary documents would be in my hands, and once they were I had to leave as quickly as possible.

I had still the journey to face, and that was not without its moments of terror. First, we travelled to Prague, with a whole party of Aryan friends who, to avert suspicion, saw me off as if it were the gayest of normal departures. We travelled on the night express from Prague to Paris, and were lucky enough to have a third class compartment to ourselves. We put our bags on the rack and each lay along the seats. In the early hours of the morning we arrived at Kehl, the border station between Germany and France, where we were awakened by shouts of, 'Alle Juden aus' (all Jews out).

'Don't you dare to move!' said Václav. We heard the Gestapo officers moving down the train for passport inspection. Our papers were inspected and handed back to us. Then came the really bloodcurdling moment when the customs officer flung open the door and shouted, 'Sind Sie ein Jude' (are you a Jew?).

'No,' said Václav casually, and I remained turned to the wall, as if sleeping. The man passed on, and the worst moment was over, but I did not draw an easy breath until we had crossed the bridge over the Rhine, and when we arrived at Strasbourg I knew we were safely in France.

I arrived in Paris in the early morning of 14 April 1939 with exactly 20 marks (£3) in my pocket, for at least in that particular I had meticulously carried out emigration instructions. Our first step was to find a very modest hotel while we looked around. Quite accidently we found just what we wanted in the artists' quarter at 125 Boulevard St Michel. It was just around the corner from where Alphonse Mucha's son, Jiří, was living in his father's studio in Rue Val de Grâce. Living with him was that extremely gifted young woman composer, Vitězslava Kaprálová, who sadly died during the war. In constant touch with them was Bohuslav Martinů, perhaps the greatest Czech composer of his day. So, from the moment of my arrival in France I was not without friends and a circle of my own. However these were difficult days for us all, and although I had friendship and sympathy it was imperative for me to find some means of earning a living as quickly as possible.

I was lucky that my cousin, Theddy, a good friend throughout my life, was working for a firm of bankers in Paris. He helped me from time to time, financially, and I was always welcome in his home. Later he disappeared into the maquis, from which he reappeared at the end of the war with the Légion d'Honneur in his buttonhole.

Of course one of my first visits was to Tcherepnin, and I cannot tell you what a wonderful tonic it was to visit that typically Russian home in Paris. At a time when every European seemed to be solely concerned with what difference total war was likely to make in his own life, this family went placidly on—their own emigration had taken place in 1917, and no modern war was going to alter their lives as the Russian Revolution had. I never succeeded in counting the members of the household; visitors came and went ceaselessly, time seemed to have little meaning, except that a meal was always in the process of preparation or dissolution. In the middle of the salon Tcherepnin himself sat at a huge table, piled with manuscripts, writing away, while around him played little groups of children. I never discovered exactly to whom they belonged, but however they laughed or cried or quarrelled he seemed to enjoy their presence, and his concentration appeared quite undisturbed.

He was kindness itself in his welcome to me, and when he realized that quite a lot of my recent experience had been with ballet in a modern theatre, he thought he probably would be able to arrange for me to work as a pianist with Colonel de Basil's Ballets Russes who were then playing in Monte Carlo. He wrote straight away, but it took some time to arrange, and while I waited I lived, as all our little circle did, on the odd engagement to accompany a dancer or singer. Many an afternoon was idled away in the Jardins de Luxembourg with a piece of bread and a bag of peanuts. Supper was apt to be a cup of coffee in an establishment where '*on reçoit avec ses provisions*'.

Of course it was wonderful to go to Monte Carlo in June, to enjoy the sunshine of the Mediterranean, to be earning one's living again, and I was certainly fortunate to be a member of such a distinguished company. But the work was hard and to a certain extent dull. In the morning I had to play relentlessly for rehearsal exercises, in the afternoon I had to practise for the piano solos I was going to play in the evening performances. I also learned what every ballet conductor will tell you, that whether you play fast or slow, interpretatively or in tempo, you may be sure that you are never quite right for the prima ballerina.

In July news began to filter through on the grapevine from Paris that the Czechs were going to form an army in exile, and this was to have its headquarters at Agde, a military harbour on the south coast of France. I threw up my job in Monte Carlo and went to Paris in order to volunteer for military service if the rumour proved to be true. Czech soldiers who had been disappointed at their fruitless mobilization during the Munich crisis were pouring into Paris to enrol in the army. I too enlisted.

While we waited for our call-up, the wife of the Czech ambassador in Paris, Paní Osuská, had borrowed a small château in Augerville de la Rivière. It was not far from Paris, and needy Czech artists, writers and musicians were given refuge there. I was given a place and found myself in good company. Mucha was there with Kaprálová, and Ivan Jelinek, the journalist. Bohuslav Martinů still lived in Paris, but often came to see us. Although we were only at Augerville for a few weeks (I joined up on 22 July and war broke out on 1 September) the time spent at this villa made a very strong impression on all who were gathered there. We were living communally under one roof and each had his own story of deprivation and homesickness, yet every day the war news caused the spirit of patriotism to grow stronger. In those short weeks we drew very close to one another, each was determined to serve his country as best he could, whether as a soldier or through his own creative art. I was already writing marches for the army that was not formed yet.

On 3 September war was declared and the rumours from Paris proved to be quite true. We were all sent from the château to Agde where some few hundred Czechs were gathered. There was already a rudimentary camp on the site, which had belonged to the Foreign Legion, but it had nothing like enough accommodation for us, and so our first task was to build barracks for the First Regiment. After about a fortnight I was sent for and commisioned to organize a military band, with the double object of inspiring the soldiers and spreading Czech propaganda among the French. A splendid idea, but the difficulties in setting about the task were almost insuperable. To begin with there was not a sheet of manuscript paper to be bought in Agde or its surroundings. I had to wait for some to be sent from Paris. The only music I could buy was a copy of Dvořák's 'Humoresque' for piano. I managed to remember, roughly, by heart, Fibich's 'Poem', and a march by Suk, and with these three pieces we began our military music.

But who were to be the instrumentalists? At the evening *rozkas* (orders for the next day) we appealed for soldiers who could play any kind of instrument. After a fortnight we had two or three violins, a cello, a bass, a trumpet, a flute and a drummer. Instruments had to be borrowed from local people, and we all met in our spare time to rehearse at the cinema where there was an upright piano. I had to write all the parts as the various musicians were added, and I well remember the excitement when we acquired a clarinet.

But my commission was to start a military band for our soldiers to march to, and somehow I had to transform this scratch orchestra into a collection of wind instruments fit to lead a column of soldiers. This was where Martinů helped us tremendously, because he found in Paris the instruments and music which had once belonged to a police band, and which the Czech consulate bought for us. One sergeant, called Mikula, had had a military band training and he helped me a great deal, rewriting all the band parts when we realized that the constitution of a

Czech band is quite different from a French one. We persevered and by January 1940 we had a full-blooded military band which was capable of performing in public concerts. The time came when we were invited to join a parade in Perpignan. It was arranged that the Czech and French bands should play alternately, but what had not been realized was that French bands play marches at 120 beats to the minute whereas the Czechs march at 116. Every time the bands changed over, either the shorter Frenchmen had to lengthen their stride, or the taller Czechs fell over their feet to get in the number of extra steps. I have yet to see a funnier sight.

By April the Germans were past the Maginot Line, but the Czech troops did not realize how the French defences had been everywhere infiltrated by the enemy, and when we were sent to the front line, north east of Paris, we hoped it was in order to hold a firm line of resistance. The fall of France came like a thunderbolt to us. In June, when Paris was occupied and Pétain's Government established, the Czech forces had orders to retreat as quickly as possible. They were to escape towards the sea and had to try to cover, if possible, 65km per day. It would be fatal for us to fall into German hands, and we could look for no support from the French.

I was in a group of thirty-six, led by a sergeant with myself as a corporal. As we made our way, some on an army truck and some on bicycles, we came across the most heartbreaking sights. The roads were often blocked by refugees, and everywhere we saw deserted farmhouses, with meals still on the table and cows bellowing to be milked. We saw many families with their babies in their arms, leading children by the hand, others pushing on handcarts all they had been able to salvage. Every now and then the German planes would zoom overhead and every man, woman and child would fall into the ditches to escape being machine-gunned. One sight I shall never forget was a railway bank with a whole row of soldiers lying dead along it in a neat unbroken line, their legionnaire caps still on their heads, machine-gunned from the air before they knew what was happening.

We crossed France in three days, snatching what little sleep we could in ditches, and reaching Bordeaux just at the time of the evacuation of Dunkirk. (This sounds an unlikely achievement, but we used any available transport and the enemy guns behind us lent wings to our feet.) We marched towards the harbour, but were told so often that we had no hope of making our escape from Bordeaux that we turned south along the coast towards Spain. Before we reached the border we came to the little fishing harbour of Arcachon, and there was a ship with quite a crowd of civilians obviously trying to get on board. With courage born of desperation, the sergeant and I forced our way on board with our field-ambulance revolvers drawn. In my case the revolver was not even loaded, and I certainly wouldn't have dared to fire it if it had been. But we managed to give the captain the impression that if he did not carry out our orders he would die on the spot. The boat was a neutral Yugoslav coaler, the *Trsat Bakar*, on its way to refill at Newport, South Wales. International law did not allow her to carry soldiers. Fortunately the captain spoke Croatian and could understand us. We told him that we were willing to change our uniforms for any clothes the sailors and civilians would lend us, and that we would hide ourselves and our uniforms in the empty coalhold. Then came the question of payment. Luckily both the sailors and the civilians were on our side and we organized a collection for some money to pay our fares. Eventually the captain set sail, but he took us far out into the Atlantic before he would set course for Newport as he was afraid of inspection by a German U-boat. All that time we had to remain hidden in the hold.

The journey lasted for several days and the question of rations soon became acute as there were about a hundred civilians besides ourselves, and the only food on board was some soup, bread and coffee, which ran out after the first two days. Consequently, when we sighted Cardiff we were pretty hungry, and very anxious as to what our reception might be. We knew our president, Beneš, was in Britain, but we had no idea what the British attitude might be to Czech soldiers escaping from French soil.

However uncertain we felt about our future, it was a wonderful feeling when we first sighted the cliffs of north Cornwall and scrambled into our uniforms. At Cardiff we reported to the port officials and all the civilians disembarked. We were given orders to sail on to Newport and stay offshore until the morning. That night we saw bombs falling on the docks. Early the next morning the army sent us some rations—loaves of bread, corned beef, tea and tinned milk. We were very glad of that food, except for the tinned milk (being slavs we didn't realize it was meant to go into the tea). Later that morning we set foot on British soil, and our welcome from the military authorities was quite a warm one. They sent trucks to convey us to Newport station, from which we went to Cholmondeley Park in Cheshire. There a message of welcome awaited us from President Beneš who was constitutional head of the Czech forces. Four years later, for my share in this little episode, to my great surprise I was awarded the Czech Military Cross.

In this dramatic fashion ends the first part of my two-part setting. How glad I was to find refuge in England! But I could not have dreamed in my wildest moments that I should build the second half of my life here, and that it would become my home.

Parents and family

Teachers:
Leo Fall (above)
Leos Janaček (above, opposite)
Josef Suk (below, opposite)

Brno Opera House

The last operetta

Czech Military Bands Mark I and Mark II
Tausky in command, France September 1939

Sergeant Tausky entertains

The Czech Army Choir singing on a
bombed site in Bermondsey as the
borough commemorated the first
anniversary of the destruction by
the Nazis of the Czech village Lidice,
June 1943

The first Promenade Concert, Royal Albert Hall 1956

The BBC Concert Orchestra

Noye's Fludde with Owen Brannigan, Towersey 1966

Home with Peggy

PART TWO

7 *A new start*

So here I was in 1940, thirty years of age, a professional musician
with the achievements I had worked so hard for behind me, in
Czechoslovakia. What help were they to me now? None at all!
In addition I had lost my family, my country and my professional
standing. One often reads of people who began their career
without a penny in their pocket, without a coat on their back.
In my case, when I landed in Britain, it was no figure of speech,
but a statement of fact, and yet the situation was worse for many
of my friends in the field ambulance who were doctors or lawyers.
If they wanted to practise their professions in this country they
had to conquer the language, and then retake their degrees in
English. My past achievements might count for nothing, but at
least what I had to offer I carried in my head. For the moment I
was housed and fed by the army, and certainly I suffered less than
many of our soldiers who were now so far away from home. I
think it was then that the home training and discipline of long
ago helped me to accept a totally new life. My wife says that my
way of dealing with difficulties is to refuse to admit they exist.
I wouldn't altogether agree with this, but I have always found it
more satisfactory to try to accept what life sends than to fight
against it.

We were drafted to the army camp at Cholmondeley Park, and
given a fortnight's freedom from duties to recover from our
ordeal on the Yugoslav coaler. It was a wonderful summer, and
the English countryside looked at its best in continental sunshine.
Our soldiers were unused to grazing country, they were accustomed to see every square metre of land used for crops. They
described the surroundings as being like one great glorious park

which didn't seem to belong to anyone. However, they soon found out that a great deal of it belonged to the young Lord Cholmondeley who lived at the castle with Lady Lettice. Both did all they could to help the Czech units, even converting an outhouse within the castle precincts into a canteen for them. They were both keen amateur musicians, and Lord Cholmondeley played piano duets with me and urged me to use the piano and organ in the castle whenever I was free to do so.

Local ladies gave parties for the Czech officers, but, as few of the regular army officers spoke English, some intelligentsia had to be fished out from the other ranks to act as interpreters. The head of the Czech forces, General Miroslav, was not himself very fluent in English and at one tea party, a lady, hovering with a silver jug, said, 'Cream, General?'

'Smetana,' quickly murmured the interpreter, translating 'cream' into Czech.

'Beautiful music, beautiful music' replied the General who thought they were talking about the composer, and the group broke up in a tangle of misunderstanding.

An even more disastrous misunderstanding happened to Lady Lettice who sent an invitation card requesting the pleasure of Captain Válek's company one Sunday afternoon. At 4 o'clock precisely, Captain Válek arrived with his company, all two hundred of them! Lady Lettice triumphed over this difficult situation magnificently. All the soldiers were taken into the canteen and given milk, apples, cigarettes, biscuits, anything that the castle or the canteen could supply, and not one left without some refreshment.

One day a group of Czech soldiers were talking to each other outside a Welsh chapel, when out popped a little Welshman and asked: 'Do you speak Welsh in your country?'

'No,' we said. 'Why should you think that?'

'We are always hearing you say "Nos da", that means "Good Night" in Welsh.'

We were actually saying 'Nazdar', which in Czech means either 'Hello' or 'Goodbye', informally.

English irony was very hard for the Czechs to understand at

first and they were not used to references to the weather being a part of every greeting. When a few days after their arrival, the postman passed the guards at the gates on his bicycle, in the pouring rain, and called out cheerily, 'Lovely day today, isn't it?' the two soldiers concluded the poor chap must be slightly mad.

At no other time in my life have I spent so many weeks, even months, when music played so small a part in my daily existence. In common with the other Czech soldiers, I was grateful for the respite from Hitler's war, and amazed and reassured by the confident attitude of British people. But perhaps we were more aware than they of how deadly was the enemy who must be encountered and defeated, if they and we were to preserve our freedom.

It was from Cholmondeley Park Camp that the Czech army was to be reorganized, and our soldiers regrouped here from countries as far afield as North Africa, Russia and Scandinavia, as well as from France and Czechoslovakia. By this time President Beneš had formed a government in exile in London and Dr Fischl, the cultural attaché, was quick to see that a propaganda department, must be set up. In 1938 Chamberlain had asked the British if they wanted to go to war on behalf of 'this distant nation of whom we know nothing'. It was now time to remedy this defect when the Czech army was on British soil and preparing to defend the freedom of both nations. At Fursecroft, George Street, London W1, the seat of the Czech Government, a department was established under Dr Fischl expressly to show all aspects of Czech culture to the wartime public of Britain.

Music played a big part in this scheme, and we musicians were given the time and opportunity to organize concerts of Czech music at every level. In Cholmondeley we reorganized the musicians of the field ambulance as our army band, and formed a Czech Army choir. Our first concerts were held in the neighbouring towns of Chester and Whitchurch where there was a colony of Czech civilians, and a day and boarding school for the children of Czech refugees. Nantwich was also very popular with the soldiers, because of a teashop there which supplied teas priced at 8d, 10d or 1s 4d (3p, 4p, 6½p). As we were paid only 6d a day,

happy the soldier who, at the end of the week, could afford the
1s 4d tea!

Distinguished professional artists from civilian life joined with
those from the army in preparing concerts of pianists, violinists
and singers and these were later heard at the Czech Institute in
London and in provincial towns all over Britain. Artists such as
Malcuzinski, Rudolph Firkušný, Maria Lonová and Liza
Fuchsová are among the names that I remember. I was responsible for many of these concerts, and the travelling involved
helped me to get to know the country and the English people, as
well as relieving the tedium of army life.

About a month after my arrival I went on leave to London. I
had no money and nowhere to stay. I was lucky. Dr Fischl's
secretary used to be at school with me, and she arranged for me
to stay in her hostel in London. It was all very unofficial and I
wasn't supposed to talk about it. But, as I later told my wife, 'I
was very comfortable there, and I had breakfast with all the girls.'
It was the YWCA.

On this leave I met two old friends from Czechoslovakia. One
was Jiří Mucha, who by now had reached London, and was
working in the Czech Information Office. The paintings of
Alphonse Mucha, his father, have recently become very fashionable again. The other old friend was Otakar Kraus, the baritone.
We recalled our first meeting, when Otakar was auditioning for
the part of Amonasro in *Aida* for Sachs at the Brno Opera House.
I was the accompanist and Sachs had a theory that no one who
needed spectacles, as Otakar did, could follow the conductor's
beat, so he sat by my side at the piano and conducted. When
Otakar had finished he said, 'And now Mr Kraus, would you
take off your glasses and go into the far corner and sing again for
me.' Still sitting at my side, Sachs reduced his beat to a miniscule
movement. However, Otakar passed triumphantly.

Neither of us imagined that in five years time we should give
together over a hundred performances of *Tosca* with the Carl
Rosa Company. Often, out of the corner of my eye, I would see
Otakar standing in the wings, quietly reading the *Evening News*,
but I knew that this apparent nonchalance would never affect his

outstanding interpretation of Scarpia. Ultimately he achieved every opera singer's lifetime ambition by appearing at La Scala, Milan. A baritone of international standing, he sang the part of Nick Shadow at the world première of *The Rake's Progress* by Stravinsky, with the composer conducting, in Venice in 1951. English audiences will remember him as Iago at Covent Garden, and as the original Tarquinius in *The Rape of Lucretia* by Britten.

One of the first places I visited on this leave, was the new Czech restaurant in Baker Street where my cousin, Gerda Ascher, was the manageress. She was the daughter of the Kaiser's counsellor, the sister of 'unser Otto', who, as I have told you, died of diphtheria in the 1914 war, and whose name I had tried to perpetuate in my youth by setting his little opera to music.

I immediately loved the atmosphere of London, although I rather agreed with Dvořák who, on one of his nine visits, said that England was delightful except for the weather and the food. Of the English, referring to their capacity for musical concentration, Dvořák said, 'It is wonderful what these people can endure. There are to be eight concerts, each of four or five hours' duration'.

But he missed his Czech food. One of the best stories Sachs told concerned the days when he was a violinist in the student orchestra of the Prague Conservatoire, and Dvořák was the principal. He enjoyed conducting for the students sometimes, and naturally, whenever he did so it was an important occasion for them. Once he was working with them on a Beethoven symphony when suddenly a reminiscent look came into his eye. He put down the baton and everyone waited eagerly for whatever pearls of wisdom would fall from his lips. 'When I was in London,' he paused reflectively, . . . 'when I was in London I found a restaurant where they served roast pork, sauerkraut and real Czech dumplings . . . Figure 27 everyone!' The baton was raised and the rehearsal continued.

This reveals the same simple mind that caused him to write home, after he had received an honorary degree of music at Cambridge University, with all the traditional ceremony that accompanies it, 'I shall never forget how I felt when they made me a doctor in England. Nothing but ceremony and nothing but doctors. All faces were serious and it seemed to me as if no one knew how to speak any other language than Latin. I looked to the right and to the left and I did not know to whom I was to listen. And when I realized that they were talking to me I had quite a shock and I was ashamed at not knowing Latin. But when I think of that today, I must laugh and I think that to compose the *Stabat Mater* was, after all, more than to know Latin.'

Even when he was quite an old man, honoured in distant lands and beloved in his own country, his simplicity was untouched. If he was not occupied in giving to the world such works as the great D Minor Symphony, he was trotting to Prague station to do some train-spotting. Once, when he was too busy to go himself, his pupil, Josef Suk, was sent. Unfortunately he made a mistake and brought back the number of the coal-tender. Dvořák turned to his daughter, who was engaged to Suk, and said scornfully, 'And you want to marry a man like that?'

We had arrived in Cheshire in June 1940 and when, in October, we were drafted to the Midlands, the soldiers were sorry to leave. They felt they could not have come to a more beautiful and peaceful spot, or to a more friendly people, to recover their strength for the struggle ahead. Now we were transferred to Leamington Spa— I, little knowing that soon I was to meet my wife and that, as a result, the second part of my career would be based in England. We were billeted at nos 17 and 19 The Parade, Leamington Spa, opposite a canteen run by the YMCA for Allied Forces, and there I met Peggy, and I was never to feel alone in England again.

The townspeople were most kind to us, but sometimes it was difficult as refugee soldiers not to feel that the hospitality offered by the upper crust of Leamington Spa was slightly patronizing— perhaps it was an inferiority complex that made us feel this. Working people who entertained us in their homes did not give us this feeling at all, but their ignorance about our country was often very disconcerting. Some even expressed surprise that we were not coloured, almost all thought that we spoke German dialect, and one soldier was asked, 'Do you have beds in Czechoslovakia?'

At which he was so annoyed that he replied, 'No, we hang from the trees by our tails.'

In the beginning I was attracted to Peggy because she was the first British woman I had met who was more interested in my ideas than in my status as a refugee soldier. For the first time, in spite of my halting English, it was as if I were talking to someone from my own background. When I visited her home, where she lived with her parents and two small sons, I felt immediately that I was welcome for myself and not as an object of compassion or patriotic charity.

Our early friendship was based on what became known as 'endless conversations' sometimes lasting deep into the night, and sometimes leading to heated argument. While we talked of music, politics, books, ballet and all the things which interested us both, I found that at this time her personal life was not much rosier than mine. Curiously enough she had strong associations with the very houses where we were billeted.

8 A soldier makes music

Although we met in 1940, it was 1 January 1948 before Peggy and I were married. 'Seven years for Rachel' as the Bible has it, but on both sides there were factors which meant that we must *festina lente* 'make haste slowly'. On Peggy's side she felt that her first responsibility was the upbringing and education of her two sons. She had not seen her husband for four years, and no satisfactory contact had been maintained. We both felt that it would be wrong to commit ourselves to any course of action until we heard his point of view. As it happened, when he did return in July 1945, he did not make claims on Peggy or the boys, so the problem was solved.

My predicament was even more involved. Although I didn't go back with the Army to Czechoslovakia, I was still in the Army, and could have been recalled at any time. Afterwards it might be difficult for me to return to England. If I married Peggy and we took the boys to Czechoslovakia, they would still be British, and their mother would be Czech. The difficulties for a family whose members had different surnames and different nationalities were fresh in our minds from the separations which occurred during the war. Another uncertainty was whether and when I should be able to obtain British nationality: without it I could not earn a living in Britain as a musician. Peggy's problem was whether she could obtain a divorce, and how long it would take. Both the granting of British nationality and of a divorce were apt, in post-war conditions, to take from two or three years to reach eventuality.

In the end I was demobilized in December 1946 and was

granted British nationality in December 1948. Peggy obtained her divorce in October 1947. We now knew that a bill was being passed through Parliament which allowed British wives marrying foreigners a choice of nationality. On 2 January 1948 the bill, by which she could reclaim British nationality, became law. So the difficulties were solved at last. We permitted ourselves one little act of bravura. We married on 1 January 1948, and Peggy became, for twenty-four hours, a Czech named Markéta Tauská. The next day she applied for British nationality.

Warwick, Stratford-upon-Avon and the nearby villages were familiar ground to Peggy for, from the age of eight until she was twenty, she had lived in the romantic village of Kenilworth, the subject of a novel by Sir Walter Scott, and an opera by Donizetti. Here almost certainly, as a boy of eleven, Will Shakespeare watched the revels held in honour of Queen Elizabeth's visit in 1575. Then the family moved to London, she married, and had two sons, who at the outbreak of the war, were aged six and two. Her first husband was sent, by British Intelligence, first to the Balkans and then to Egypt, but not before his masters had seen that Peggy and the two children were placed at the very centre of England in what they considered to be an inner ring of security, should there be an invasion.

So she came back to Kenilworth, where, unbelievable as it seems today, she lived in a very pleasant private hotel in the prettiest part of the village, with a private sitting room and bathroom, two bedrooms and four excellent meals a day at a charge of six guineas a week for the three of them.

In the Autumn of 1940 they moved into Leamington Spa, so that Nicholas, the older boy, could go to school. Peggy began teaching at Kingsley school where she had been a pupil herself. Formerly the school had occupied two attractive Regency houses on the Parade. Later it was transferred to Beauchamp Hall, and the original houses stood empty for many years. When the Czech Field Ambulance came to Leamington they were quartered in these very houses. I still find it both amazing and romantic that I should arrive in Leamington Spa to sleep in the very classrooms where Peggy had been taught as a child.

The Czech soldiers were as well received in Leamington as they had been in Cheshire, and it was not long before they were joining in what social life there was during wartime.

Peggy became friendly with a man who had made the law his profession, then changed it to become a cellist, and now found himself a private in the Czech Army. Opposite the Czech billets on the Parade was the YMCA canteen run by local ladies for the soldiers who found it very handy, as even when they were on duty they could pop across the road for a quick coffee, or a packet of cigarettes. Musicians spent whatever leisure time they had there, as there were both upright and grand pianos and also upstairs rooms where instrumentalists could practise. One day Neumann, the cellist, who spent a good deal of time pouring out his miseries to me, said, 'I would like you to meet a friend of mine. Will you come to the YMCA canteen at 6 o'clock, and I shall bring her to meet you?'

The friend was Peggy, and she has often told me how I struck her as having very blue eyes and very red cheeks, with black curly hair, very solid and trustworthy looking. I remember what she said to me on that occasion: 'Are you a musician too? You look more like a farmer.' We all got on famously together, although the evening ended in a heated discussion between Peggy and me. She said, 'I like your Czech soldiers with their slanty eyes and their no-good-boyo faces!'

I replied, 'You only look at the officers, they are stupid fellows. It is only "our boys" who are serious.'

The next time I met her was at a St Nicholas' Day dance where I presented her with a St Nicholas made in gingerbread which highly delighted her, being so typically Czech. From then on she took me on a series of outings in Shakespeare country. Stratford-upon-Avon, Mary Arden's house, Kenilworth, Guy's Cliffe, Warwick, we visited them all. Peggy still teases me about how, after one particularly exhausting expedition, I sank into a chair at the Hathaway tea rooms, saying to the waitress, 'Big jugs of coffee and hundreds of breads and butters.'

Czech units were formed at Wellesbourne, Kineton and Walton Hall, as well as at Leamington where a cultural liaison office was established. The arrangements, which had been tried out in Cheshire, to promote Czech music were now able to be used far more extensively. The Army band played in Coventry, Rugby, Nuneaton and many other Midland towns and army camps, I was kept busy making arrangements of folk and national Czech music for the band and choir. 'The Czechs are marching', 'Waltzing through Czechoslovakia,' and 'Under Czech Skies' bring in many an honest penny to this day, through the Performing Right Society. In preparation for Christmas 1941, I made an arrangement of eight Czech carols, the proceeds of which were donated to the Czech Red Cross. That little book has been used in hundreds of British schools ever since.

A great feature of those days was the concerts of Czech music given in English country houses for wartime charities. As far as the Czechs were concerned, it was an excellent opportunity to promote their music, and use some of the fine professional artists at their disposal. The British used it as a chance to raise some money for the war effort, and to enjoy the social occasion, which was justified by its aims. The results were sometimes funnier than either side was able to realize.

By this time Peggy was president of the Anglo-Czech Friendship Club in Leamington, and attended some of the concerts in that capacity. On one such occasion she and a Czech lady were deputed to go ahead and make the arrangements for a Sunday afternoon concert and tea, to be held at a beautiful English country house outside Stratford. On the way she was briefed by the very forceful Czech lady who was her opposite number, 'When we get there I will speak, you shall be silent. You are here just to represent the English. I will talk, I am more experienced in these matters.'

Peggy foolishly let her have her way. They were received by our hostess, all graciousness, 'I thought, ladies, we could use *this* little room for the exhibition of Czech folk art.'

'No,' replied Peggy's companion, 'this will not do, it is too small, and also too ugly.' You can imagine Peggy's feelings!

But the Czechs had some surprises coming too. On my arrival I was handed over to the lady in charge of the music, a local patroness of the arts. Taking a trio by Beethoven, which it was proposed we play, she flicked over the pages rapidly, 'We'll begin here . . . we'll cut this bit . . . we only want that much of the slow movement . . . and we had better finish here.' Swiftly she tore it to ribbons. We had not enough English to argue, and aghast, but helpless, we obediently played it in this mutilated form.

Maria Lonová, the violinist of the Czech trio, told me she had played Dvořák's 'Humoresque' arranged for violin about 250 times, as it was the one piece that all British people recognized as Czech. At this particular concert our host approached her, nervously fingering his Old Etonian tie, 'I say, that was wonderful,' he said. 'One doesn't know how you keep it up, don't your fingers sometimes get tired?' Then turning to me who had accompanied her, and obviously feeling that I must not be left out he said, 'I thought you played frightfully well too, old chap!' I really didn't know what to make of this form of congratulation. I should understand better today!

I wondered why, in private houses, everyone murmured 'thank you' at the end of each piece, like 'Amen, amen!' Peggy said, 'It's the custom when people are playing for friends. What would you say at home when a piece finishes?'

'Oh, you might comment on what had been played, or suggest what should follow, but we never reverently murmur "Thank you".'

On another Sunday Peggy was unable to go to a concert of the same kind and, meeting my friend, the cellist, who had been playing there, she said, 'How did it go this afternoon?'

'Oh, better, I think,' he said. 'The choir sang a few vulgar songs, and that cheered things up.' Vulgar songs in that aristocratic atmosphere—the mind boggled! Then she realised that 'vulgar' songs to him, were 'folksongs' to the British.

These were some of the funnier moments in learning to understand each other, but on the whole the British were very appreciative of the chance to hear music by Smetana, Dvořák, Janáček and Martinů, of whose work they knew little, and it made a great difference that they could hear performances by Czech musicians.

In London, Jaroslav Knapp, secretary of the pre-war Czech Institute at 6 Grosvenor Square, was doing much to provide a wide audience of both British and Czech people with concerts, lectures and exhibitions of Czech art. I was sent to London to prepare and conduct concert versions of Czech operas. Among these were *The Kiss*, *Dalibor*, *Libuše* and *The Two Widows* by Smetana. This last, an enchanting comedy, has still not been given a professional stage performance in Britain. *Rusalka* and *Jacobin* by Dvořák were also heard for the first time in Britain.

In these operas I had to work with very uneven casts. Some of the singers were professionals of high standing, and others had good voices but little operatic experience. One British lady, married to a Czech, was rather lacking in imagination, and felt quite at sea among these professionals when she was given the part of the witch in *Rusalka*. She did her rather stolid best, but Peggy told me afterwards that I hadn't improved matters by bellowing at her in desperation, 'I don't vant Mrs Tomašov of St Albans. I vant a vitch!'

As well as the operas, there were concerts of chamber-music. An inspired idea of Jaroslav Knapp was a concert at which the Czech Army Choir and the Fleet Street Choir sang, in turn, groups of their native folksongs. Poetry readings were also exchanged, and at one of these, arranged by the PEN Club, I was asked to write incidental music for a reading of T. S. Eliot's poem *East Coker*, and I still treasure the copy inscribed for me by the author.

At this time I was in London sometimes as often as twice a week. These activities meant many contacts with civilian life for me, although I was always under military discipline and had, at a prescribed hour, to return to a waterlogged army camp, often to sleep on the floor or in a crowded train. In spite of these restrictions I met and worked with many well known musicians who were also employed in keeping culture alive in wartime Britain. Among them were Dennis Brain, Eric Harrison, Fred Grinke, Cyril Smith, Harriet Cohen and many others.

In Leamington, Arthur German, the nephew and heir of

Edward German, and his wife, Mary, made me welcome in their home at all times. They had a beautiful grand piano which was always at my disposal. I used to enjoy playing piano duets with Mary, and when we had made a mistake I used to say, in my limited English, 'Let's begin upstairs, shall we?' meaning at the top of the page. I could never understand why she always laughed at this, until one day she could no longer resist explaining, and said, 'That proposal is open to misunderstandings!'

Only last year, at a concert in Solihull, I met Mrs Matthews, the mother of Dennis. She had brought a party of people from Leamington, who remembered me from the old days. Dennis was then only about seventeen, but already a fantastic musician with a prodigious musical memory. Mrs Matthews, who did so much in his early days to promote his career, said how glad she had been for him to have the company of these mature musicians. We recalled many happy evenings of music, when she kept open house, and I assured her how much her sympathy and hospitality had meant to us. Dennis and I have kept in touch for over thirty years. On one of my trips to London, through Maria Lonová, I met Felix Aprahamian, now a music critic for *The Sunday Times*. He was then secretary of the London Philharmonic Orchestra which was managed by Tom Russell. Felix waved a magic wand and I could hardly believe it when I learnt that I was to conduct the London Philharmonic with Benno Moiseiwitsch as soloist. The chances of an unknown conductor securing a concert with a first class orchestra were as unlikely then as now. I have always regarded this as an outstanding example of how my best chances are always unsought. The concert took place at the Orpheum, Golders Green on 28 February 1942. Moiseiwitsch played Rachmaninov's 2nd Piano Concerto, and the concert finished with Dvořák's 'New World' Symphony.

Perhaps as a result of this concert, Walter Legge of ENSA and CEMA concerts invited me to conduct, and eventually I became one of their leading conductors. These concerts usually took the form of popular symphonic concerts, with pianists such as Solomon, Eileen Joyce or Louis Kentner as soloists. David Wise, Marie Wilson and Henry Holst often appeared as violinists.

Joan Hammond, Nancy Evans and Heddle Nash were popular as singers. In all I gave over 200 of these concerts for warworkers, which were held in factories, canteens, town halls and army camps all over the country. The following account of my appearance at Watford town hall on 10 August 1943 gives the feeling of those wartime concerts:

Sergeant Tausky, leader of the Czechoslovak Army Choir, has endeared himself to the concert-going public by his genial ways and by his hearty treatment of music, both light and serious. He is indeed a born musician.

Apart from his army activities Tausky has taken a lively interest in the musical life of Britain, and was incidentally the first foreigner to conduct the band of the Coldstream Guards. Quite recently he conducted the London Philharmonic Orchestra in Bristol and was warmly welcomed there by public and press. On Tuesday 10 August, Tausky and the London Philharmonic performed in Watford. They played in the crowded town hall a popular programme of Smetana, Dvořák, Grieg and Ravel.

We went to see Tausky in the artist's room soon after he had led his orchestra to the final din of Ravel's *Bolero*. Tired and elated he was changing his third shirt (conducting is hard work) and discussing his horn player—the best horn player he said, he had worked with for years. [This was not surprising as it was Dennis Brain.] He also spoke highly of the orchestra as a whole and praised its diligence, good will and spirit of collaboration.

There were a good many Allied soldiers in the concert hall, and as we were leaving Tausky was confronted by a lorry full of enthusiastic Canadians who hailed him, and had their programmes signed. So he set to work again. The lorry held forty-three passengers by the way, as one of the Canadians explained. As they cheered him on ('Come on, Mr Tausky, there are only four left!') a gurgly voice from behind said, 'Hi, Mr Tausky, what about an American soldier?'

After having conducted the Czechoslovak Army Choir in the Albert Hall two days later, Tausky and the London Philharmonic Orchestra left London to fulfill a series of engagements in the provinces.

The *Evening News* also reported that the Coldstream Guards, giving a concert of Czech music to the Royal Navy, broke a 260 year old tradition by following the baton of a foreign conductor. The occasion, which included hospitality on a destroyer, complete with a piping aboard, was quite outstanding.

For the anniversary of the occupation of Czechoslovakia I was invited by the Anglo-Czech Friendship Club of Liverpool to conduct a performance of Smetana's *Má Vlast* (My Country), a work which was banned in Czechoslovakia during the German occupation. The Liverpool Philharmonic was the first British orchestra to give a performance of the complete cycle.

Despite my constant absence on musical duties I was still based at 17 The Parade, Leamington Spa, when the great raid on Coventry occurred. The Czech Field Ambulance was rushed there in the small hours of the morning to give what help it could. I was deeply moved by the whole experience and, within a few days, had written my string quartet 'Coventry'. Before I left Czechoslovakia my teacher, Josef Suk, had advised me, 'If ever you write music in England you must send it to my old friend, Sir George Dyson'.

This I proposed to do, and asked Peggy to help me with the letter. I was very keen to begin 'Dear Sir Dyson', just as Beethoven once began 'Dear Sir Smart', to Sir Frederick Smart the president of the Royal Philharmonic Society. When Peggy suggested gently that it should be 'Dear Sir George', I said, 'But Peggy, I can't call him by his Christian name, I don't know him'. However I was persuaded, and later we heard that Sir George had said, on perusing the score, 'Here, at last, is something that sounds like music'.

Sir George passed it to Myra Hess who included it in the famous lunchtime National Gallery concerts, when it was played by the Menges Quartet. I was very proud when the advertised programme for Tuesday 17 March read 'Tausky and Beethoven', feeling that at least I was in good company.

About this time there was a visit of President Beneš, accompanied by Mr Churchill, to the Czech troops at Walton Hall. President Beneš told the soldiers, 'You have come from many different countries, some of you have fled from country to country, but I promise you this is the end—from this country you will go home.'

When Churchill was ready to leave, the Czech Army Choir broke into 'Rule Britannia' and there were tears in his eyes—this, I believe, was a fairly common occurrence, for he was an emotional man. Nevertheless, this very English tune, sung in vigorous Slav accents, by soldiers who could only just manage the words, was a moving experience for all who heard it.

I had much the same feeling, but in reverse, on a glorious summer day in 1942, when the war news was at its worst. Kingsley School was kept open in the summer holidays because so many parents were on war work and, for the purposes of morale, every morning ended in an informal singsong. I was walking along a deserted side street in the sunshine thinking to myself, 'We shall win in the end, we *must* win . . . but how shall we win, that's the question?' Suddenly, over the high grey wall, came the sound of a hundred girls' voices singing with immense conviction, 'There'll always be an England!'

'Perhaps that's the answer,' I thought, and went on my way cheered. Many years later, when I returned to Leamington to talk to the girls of Kingsley school, my subject was the development of taste in music. I told them this story of the Kingsley girls to illustrate that it is not always the greatest music that is necessarily the right music, or the most moving, at a particular moment. The song that I heard over the wall was only a popular tune, but it just happened to carry the right message at the right moment. In music, as in other matters, the heart must sometimes be allowed to prevail.

During 1943 I was given three months leave of absence from the Army to write the music for a film *Interim Balance*, the history of the Czech Army exile in France and England. Jan Masaryk, who was about to go to America as Czechoslovakian Foreign Minister, sent for me before he left. 'What can I do for you?' he asked. 'You are doing so much for Czechoslovakia.'

'Bring me a fountain pen from America that I can write music with,' I replied promptly. I had to wait two years for that pen, but Jan Masaryk didn't forget, and I use it to this day.

Despite the destruction of the Queen's Hall by bombing, the Promenade Concerts continued to cheer the wartime population from their new home at the Royal Albert Hall. During one season, conducted mainly by Sir Adrian Boult, fortnightly concerts were devoted to music of the Allies. Scott Goddard of the *News Chronicle*, commenting on the Czech Army Choir, which I conducted, said, 'A set of songs for unaccompanied male voices was magnificently sung by the Czech Army Choir. First, the great Ploughing Song, which to a man of that country portrays not one field, but the whole land. The last was a dramatic episode in the Hus chronicle, also by Smetana, which sounded very stirring when performed with the vigour and vitality heard last night.'

And now, at last came the beginning of the end, in June 1945— the long awaited invasion. The journey homeward promised by President Beneš had begun, and the Czech contingent left England as part of Montgomery's army. On the night before entrainment, I developed a serious pneumonic infection of the throat, and was left behind with a temperature of 104 degrees. Within a day or two I was transferred to an Army hospital in Driffield, Yorkshire, where I was very ill for some weeks.

Two months later I was attached to the remnant of Czech Army HQ at Piccadilly, and here I occupied myself with office work when I wasn't involved in making music. Before General Miroslav left England, I had been promoted to the rank of 2nd lieutenant and awarded the Czechoslovak Order of Merit, which I received from the General himself. When the provisional Czech Government left for Prague, a farewell concert was given in honour of the President and his ministers. This concert, which I arranged and conducted, took place at Westminster Central Hall, in the presence of Allied ambassadors. The orchestra was the

London Philharmonic, the soloists were Liza Fuchsova, in Dvořák's Piano Concerto, and Maria Lonová in Suk's 'Violin Fantasy'. The farewell oration was spoken by Jan Masaryk.

Although I was in uniform until 1946 the war, as a fighting war, was by now over for me. I hope that this chapter will have shown that through my varied musical activities in war-time Britain I had already made many contacts which ultimately helped me to begin a career in this country.

9 The Carl Rosa

In June 1945, after VE Day, those of us who remained at the Piccadilly headquarters were all thinking of demobilization and whether we should return to Czechoslovakia or stay on in Britain. For me, there were three possibilities.

I could still return home, demobilize there, and see what professional chances were open to me, even though I had already found out that there was no place for me at Brno Opera House. Had I returned I would have asked Peggy to come there with the children when I was, to some degree, established. That plan was obviously very long term and too vague.

I could apply for British nationality and hope to build a career in England, but naturalization could take as long as five years, and it was difficult for a foreigner to obtain a work permit.

I could also, if I wanted, take up the affadavit that my brother, who had emigrated to Canada, could procure for me. In this case I would be granted British nationality after six months' residence in Canada, when I could return to Britain. I turned over all these possibilities in my mind, and was slightly inclined to favour the last. In the meantime I took out naturalization papers in Britain as it was likely to be a long process. However, the matter was settled without question by a 'bolt from the blue'— as has always been the case throughout my life.

For some time I had held the conviction that there was work for me to do in this world and that this work would come to me without my seeking it. I described earlier with what horror I saw the row of machine-gunned legionnaires in France during an overhead air attack by the Luftwaffe. At the height of the attack

I ran to shelter in a deserted house, felt unsafe in case the roof fell in, ran into the garden and flung myself flat among the fruit bushes. When the attack subsided and I saw the devastation around me I felt an overwhelming conviction, at a deeper level than that of reason, that my life had been saved for some purpose. From that time onward I have believed that I should do gladly the work that comes my way.

I had the same experience once again later in the war. One day, during the doodlebug raids I was walking to the Wigmore Hall, past the Times Bookshop, when I heard one cut out overhead. I dodged into the shop entrance and after the bomb had exploded, very near indeed, I realized what a silly place I had chosen to shelter, for I was completely surrounded by glass. The entrance was unshattered, although there was plenty of broken glass around. Again, I had the same total certainty that I was saved by a power, which would also mould my future.

The next thing that happened to me was a complete justification of these feelings. Quite unexpectedly, in the summer of 1945, while I was still undecided as to where my future would lie, I had a letter from Mr H. B. Phillips of the Carl Rosa Opera Company, saying that they were reorganizing the company and would I like to become its musical director, mentioning a generous salary. There it was, his definite offer. No suggestion that we should talk over the possibility, or even that I should conduct some performances first! I shall never know how this idea came to the Phillips or what they knew of my capabilities. By that time I had conducted a great deal of symphonic music in England, but I had had little opportunity to conduct opera.

I went to see Mrs Phillips, who was the artistic director of the company, and she explained that they wanted to improve the orchestra, look for new young singers, and in every way upgrade the company's standard after their wartime improvizations.

In those days Covent Garden was closed, and Sadler's Wells was running on a shoestring budget, filling part of the season with wartime touring. Carl Rosa had a good tradition as the only permanent touring opera company in England, and had a yearly season in London at the Winter Garden Theatre and later at the King's Theatre, Hammersmith.

Carl Rosa, a German violinist, had first formed his touring opera company in 1875 and very good standards had since been maintained for over sixty years. The Carl Rosa toured all the major cities as far north as Aberdeen, Edinburgh and Glasgow, and as far west as Plymouth, Exeter and Bristol. They were particularly popular in the larger industrial towns of the north, where there was a great choral tradition, and people were especially appreciative of well produced opera which the Carl Rosa was the first company to produce in Britain. They had been responsible for the first performance of Wagner's *Ring*, and Puccini himself had attended the first *La Bohème* in Manchester. Many of the standard operas of the day, as well as a number of first performances by British composers, had been produced by this company. Nothing could have suited me better than to be invited to direct one of the only two opera companies existing in Britain at this time.

Following my first interview with Mrs Phillips, I had an appointment with her husband at the Waldorf Hotel and there I accepted his offer. It was only then that he invited me to go with him to see a performance of *Tosca* at Southsea, the first opera that they wanted me to take over. I was pleased at the high standard of the performance. The three principals were Joan Hammond, Otakar Kraus and John Myrddin. The two first artists are talked of elsewhere, but John Myrddin was a Welsh miner who had a voice of outstanding beauty and could certainly have become a singer of international standing. Later in his career Bruno Walter was to offer him a position as Heldentenor in Germany, but his home and family came first. I met him many years later in Cardiff where he was very happy as a member of the BBC chorus.

Mr and Mrs Phillips were a fascinating couple to work for. If ever there was an indissoluble marriage which was both personally and professionally based on a love-hate relationship, this was it. Neither could do without the other, either in life or in work; each was a gifted person, their gifts complemented each other, and yet neither could bear to acknowledge the sphere in which the other was paramount.

Mr Phillips was a very shrewd businessman, and his iron hand on finances controlled Mrs Phillips' excellent, but extravagant, ideas on production. 'He is very good on the box office side, but his idea of opera is the Soldiers' Chorus from *Faust*,' she was apt to say in derogatory tones.

On the other hand her particular weakness was for intrigue within the company, which she didn't confine to the spoken word. On one occasion she wrote me a particularly scurrilous letter alleging personal favouritism in casting, and I thought it best to take it direct to Mr Phillips, who was very straightforward in all his dealings. 'Shall I show you what I do when I receive a letter like this?' he said, and very neatly he tore it up into small pieces which fluttered into the wastepaper basket. I understood that he had learned wisdom the hard way, and not another word passed between us.

He showed equal judgement when, one day, a prima donna stormed into his room, complaining that her dress had been borrowed by another singer without permission and not even sent to the cleaners afterwards. She proceeded to go into vivid detail as to how she was unable to wear it as it smelt. 'I am used to working with ladies, Mr Phillips,' she ended.

'So am I,' replied Mr Phillips quietly, but with point.

Every member of the company spoke of him in the same way: 'When you deal with Mr Phillips you are dealing with a gentleman'. He always kept his word, and was scrupulously fair in his dealings with his employees. On the other hand, he did keep a tight hand on the money bags. After I had been with the company for some weeks I persuaded him, reluctantly, to let us have a tuba for the Verdi and Puccini operas. Unfortunately, the week after the tuba player joined us, the operas were *Faust*, *Carmen* and *The Tales of Hoffman*. On Friday, fresh from having paid the salaries, Mr Phillips met me in the corridor. 'Fifteen pounds for a tuba', he growled, 'and he hasn't played a note yet.'

Mrs Phillips strove for years to achieve the acknowledged title of artistic director for which her talent really suited her, but Mr

Phillips was always afraid that this would lead to her usurping other powers. In this he was probably right—she was a great lady for power. In her turn, she went round saying to members of the company: 'He's really past the touring, you know, he should let me take over'.

She had a great theatrical flair for recognizing talent in a raw young soprano and predicting the roles she would be able to develop: she was nearly always right. She would promote these singers, and give them every kind of help and backing. However, once the singer was established and began to gain confidence, and particularly if the girls began to try out a few prima donna airs, Mrs Phillips would turn against them and another fledgling would become the new favourite. Nobody had a keener eye for detail on the stage than she. God help the Marguerite who forgot to remove her wedding ring before she went on stage! She had a sharp eye for the company's property too and was once heard to hiss from the auditorium to Donald Campbell, the bass, as he tossed his hat in the air, 'Careful with that hat, it cost £30!'

When I first came to the company, the musical director was Charles Webber who was nearly seventy, and ready to retire. He was a very efficient and experienced operatic conductor, and was able at many points to help me with the differences between my Continental experience and the way this British touring company was run. With the passing of the years, Charlie had developed his own eccentricities, and very funny some of them were. One was a tendency to take the audience into his confidence. As the more tricky moments in certain arias approached, he would turn his head slightly over his shoulder, and say to the audience, 'She doesn't know the next bit,' and a minute or so later, 'Wrong again'. But the general scope of his work was so good that no one took any notice of these unconventional little asides.

My first performance with Carl Rosa was *Tosca* at Wimbledon Theatre on 20 November 1945, with the same cast I had heard at Southsea. This performance made me feel confident that I should be able to establish a good rapport with the artists and orchestra in the company. After the performance I met Otakar Kraus in the underground, with a lady who had obviously been at the performance. He said: 'This is our new musical director, Vilem Tausky . . . Miss Eva Turner.'

'How do you do?' I said politely.

Otakar gave me a look and a nudge and repeated, 'Miss Eva Turner'.

Still the penny didn't drop. The lady smiled, 'He means "Ayva TOURR-NER",' she said. Of course it was a name that every international opera lover knew, but I had not recognized it pronounced in BBC English. I am proud to say that she still regularly attends our operatic performances at the Guildhall School. Dame Eva began her career in the Carl Rosa and went from there to La Scala, where eventually she sang the première of Puccini's *Turandot* with Toscanini. Later, in London, Eva sang the role at Covent Garden under Constant Lambert with Walter Midgley as the tenor. Later still she sang for me at Covent Garden when Kinasiewicz was the Turandot.

Very often singers have speaking voices which are quite different from their singing voices. This was not so with Walter who had such a high pitched voice in real life that when he answered the telephone people had been known to say, 'Good afternoon, Mrs Midgley, could I speak to Walter?'

In the old days at Covent Garden a call boy went the rounds of the dressing rooms calling, 'Quarter of an hour, Mr Midgley . . . Five minutes, Mr Midgley . . .'. Returning the third time to see Walter still putting the final touches to his make up, he exclaimed agitatedly, 'Mr Midgley, you're on!'

And a high tenor voice squeaked out, 'Am I, how'm I doing?'

I was fortunate on joining the company to have Joan Hammond to sing Tosca, Madame Butterfly, Marguerite and Violetta. In addition to an exceptionally beautiful voice and distinguished stage presence, she cared deeply about every note of the music. I can honestly say that I have never known a singer who loved the music of the opera so much for its own sake as Joan did. She was the greatest perfectionist and expected the same high standards from all her colleagues as she gave herself. Of course this helped to raise the standard of any performance in which she was concerned. In *Tosca*, for instance, during the highly dramatic ending, Joan had to cast herself down from the battlements, and she was rightly concerned that this should look convincing. Naturally, she was not able to jump with the necessary abandon unless the offstage mattresses on which she had to fall were in exactly the right position. If they were not perfectly arranged, Joan did not hesitate to hold an inquest on those responsible. Eventually, the stage hands grew tired of this and decided to have their own back, so they placed a trampoline under the mattresses and, that night, after her dramatic leap, Joan reappeared once or twice, gently bouncing above the battlements. No one enjoyed a joke more than Joan, for she had a tremendous sense of humour but I doubt if she approved of jokes during a performance, although offstage she was herself a great leg-puller.

I enjoyed every show I did with Joan, and am very proud of the records I made with her, especially of the Moon song from *Rusalka* by Dvořák, which was hitherto unknown, and is now famous throughout the world. It was a sad day for music when Joan's brilliant career was cut short by heart trouble. I fear she had worked too hard and had given too unsparingly of herself. She was advised to retire to the warm climate of her native Australia. Peggy and I still miss our visits to the Old Cottage, Little Egypt-on-the-Nile, Burnham Beeches, where we had many happy times. There we came to know Lolita and Essie, her two friends and secretaries, whom, after her appearance as Rusalka, we christened ' The attendant sprites'. Everyone in the world of music, as well as thousands of her fans, was delighted when, in 1973, Joan was created a dame of the British Empire, a title which was greatly deserved.

A pair of singers whom I enjoyed working with in my early days with the Rosa were Helen Ogilvie and Gladys Parr, as Chochosan and Suzuki in *Madame Butterfly*. Although they were approaching retirement when I joined the company, they still gave a marvellous performance in these roles. Gladys was well known for her work at Covent Garden with Sir Thomas Beecham before the war; perhaps one of her best roles was Nicklaus in *The Tales of Hoffman*. Britten chose her to sing Florence in the première of *Albert Herring*, and also Mrs Noah in *Noye's Fludde*.

Then there was another pair of well established English opera singers, Tudor Davies and his wife, Ruth Packer. By the time I arrived they were only appearing with the company as guest artists, but Tudor sang the title role in *The Tales of Hoffman*, and he was magnificent. Ruth sang Leonora in *Il Trovatore* with me, and a memorable *La Traviata*, when she stepped in at a few hours notice in a part that she had not sung for some years. When I did *The Kiss* by Smetana, Ruth played the heroine, Vendulka. At that time she must have been over forty, and the part she was taking was that of a young Czech girl, too shy to grant her fiancé the kiss that will seal their bargain. Both vocally and in appearance, Ruth played this part with great charm, and with her two long plaits and simple peasant dress looked about half her age.

After I had been there a few months, the Phillips engaged a new young conductor to help me, Peter Gellhorn. David Ellenberg was already on the staff, both were good musicians and we worked together for most of the three years I was there. Peter later went on to become a coach at Covent Garden, chorus master at Glyndebourne and ultimately the director of the BBC chorus.

We gave a fortnight's season in most of the major cities and a week in some of the smaller ones. This repertoire of a week's performances in Oxford is an example of how we worked and of the artists and variety of opera we offered.

Advance publicity for the Carl Rosa Opera at the New Theatre Oxford March 10th - 15th 1947

Monday	*Madame Butterfly*	Joan Hammond, recently returned from a triumphant recital tour of Australia and New Zealand. Shortly to appear in grand opera in Vienna
Tuesday	*Rigoletto*	Gwen Catley, star of radio and gramophone, Joseph Satariano as Rigoletto, Norman Allin, England's great bass

Wednesday matinee	*Cavalleria Rusticana* *I Pagliacci*	All star cast: Joan Hammond, Arthur Fear
Wednesday evening	*La Bohème*	Otakar Kraus, Norman Allin
Thursday	*Tales of Hoffman*	Conductor: Warwick Braithwaite
Friday	*La Tosca*	Gaby Vallé
Saturday matinee	*Madame Butterfly*	
Saturday evening	*Faust*	Joan Hammond Ronald Stear as Mephistopheles

A noteworthy feature of the Carl Rosa ensemble is the orchestra, entirely composed of musicians travelling with the Company; and mention must be made of another famous conductor who is in charge of the musical side of several operas. This is Vilem Tausky, who before the war was conductor at Brno Opera. He came to this country, having seen active service abroad as a lieutenant in the Czechoslovakian army, and on the cessation of hostilities was engaged by the Carl Rosa.

As well as these well known names, Mrs Phillips and I were trying to graft new talent into the company. One girl, who started in the chorus, became one of the best known British opera singers during the next twenty years. Another came to us from the Royal Academy and Sadler's Wells, where she was in the chorus and took small parts. After some distinguished performances with the Rosa she joined the Royal Opera House. They were Victoria Elliott and Blanche Turner.

Victoria Elliott had an outstandingly good dramatic soprano voice, and a great sense of how much hard work it takes to achieve and maintain a position as a principal soprano. While she was still in the chorus she was always to be found standing in the wings listening to Joan Hammond, Helen Ogilvie or Ruth Packer. She was determined to learn these roles, and she succeeded. Came the day when Joan was unable to go on as Marguerite, Victoria aged twenty-two took her place with great success. A little later the same thing happened with *La Bohème*, and again Vicki knew the music and the production; this time her performance was a resounding success, and from then on she gradually became a principal soprano with the Rosa. Later she was a principal for many years at Sadler's Wells. After a break, when she studied for some months in Italy, she sang Leonora (*Il Trovatore*) at Covent Garden. She also created the role of Lady Hamilton in Lennox Berkeley's *Nelson*. She was one of the hardest working singers I have ever known, and the secret of her success, from a conductor's point of view, was that she was musically completely reliable and always gave of her best.

Blanche Turner had a dramatic soprano voice of great power and beauty. She sang Musetta to Vicki's Mimi, and also *Tosca* and *La Traviata*. Blanche was an accomplished operatic actress, but her trouble was that she never liked the roles she was given and, having done an excellent Micaela or Musetta, she would burst out, 'I hate myself in that part'. I don't know why this was, and I really don't think she did either. Britten had her in mind when he wrote one of the nieces in *Peter Grimes*, and this she did actually admit she enjoyed singing.

Blanche had the very vivid imagination necessary for an opera singer who so often has to convince an audience of situations far removed from everyday life. Her talent in this direction was sometimes apt to spill over into her personal life and we all knew that some of her stories had to be taken with a pinch of salt. On one occasion she was singing Blonde in *Il Seraglio* at the Garden, and in this production Blonde wore Victorian pantelettes. Blanche rang us up early the next morning. 'Oh, my dears, what a tragedy, my pants fell down on stage! Fortunately the lighting man saw I was in difficulty and put me into darkness, and I stepped neatly out of them, but I had to finish the scene with them draped over my arm.'

It happened that, later that day, I was coaching Kenneth Neate, the tenor who had been singing opposite her the night before. 'How unfortunate about Blanche's pants last night!' I said. 'It must have been rather embarrassing.'

'Oh, what happened?' said he. 'I never noticed anything.'

I may say the story was as typical of Ken as it was of Blanche, for he never noticed anything when he was on stage except what was happening to 'the Voice', as he called it—his own!

My guess is that nothing more serious happened than that Blanche was aware of a loosened elastic.

I will not attempt to give you a detailed account of the work I did with the Rosa between 1946–9; it would be as boring as if I had written in detail about ten years in Brno. It is enough to say that during this time I conducted about a hundred and fifty performances each of *Madame Butterfly* and *La Bohème*, a hundred each of *Il Trovatore* and *Rigoletto*, besides many of *Faust*, *Cavalleria Rusticana*, *I Pagliacci* and *The Tales of Hoffman*. During the three years I also prepared and conducted three new productions for the company, each of which was exciting for me in a different way.

The first year we did *Carmen*. Mrs Phillips had found in Janet Howe a spectacular singer for the title role. There have been Carmens whose vocal powers were more luscious, but hers were very adequate and, when added to her great beauty and dramatic personality, were just what the part needed. Janet wore the provocative clothes designed by Hamish Wilson with supreme panache. She studied the role with one of the most famous Carmens, Madame Lussan, then living in London in retirement. Instead of the castanets being played from the orchestra, Janet learned to play them herself, and used them to great effect. My own particular satisfaction was in the famous quintet in the second act, which I think you would seldom hear better sung.

The next year we did *The Flying Dutchman*, produced by Harry Powell Lloyd, and this was the beginning of an enormously satisfactory association between us, which continued in later productions at Sadler's Wells, and in the Dublin Grand Opera Society. Edna Hobson, a well established singer from the North Country, was our Senta. Unfortunately she fell ill after a few performances, but Blanche Turner took over the role very ably. The Dutchman was sung first by Arthur Fear, and then by Tom Williams from Sadler's Wells. Powell Lloyd designed beautiful sets, with an intricate arrangement in the last scene by which, at a certain point in the score, the ship slowly sank as the sun rose. As we passed from theatre to theatre, not all of them with adequate stage equipment, there was always a certain amount of doubt as to whether there would be perfect synchronization between the conductor, the stage staff and the lighting man. Harry, who was of a naturally pessimistic outlook, used to hold his head in his hands before every performance, murmuring, 'They ask impossibilities, old chap, they ask impossibilities'. But the ending usually did come off and, when it did, was a breathtaking effect and worth all the anxiety.

The last production I did with the Rosa was for me the most exciting: *The Kiss* by Smetana, never before given professionally in Britain. Mrs Phillips was quite interested in putting it on, as she had seen the success of *The Bartered Bride* at the Wells, and I spurred her on by talking of the fine tradition the Rosa had in the past for first productions of operas in English. Jaroslav Knapp, whose fine work for the Czech Institute during the war I have mentioned before, made the translation with the help of his English wife. Hamish Wilson designed the most delightful and authentic sets, and some of the beautiful national costumes were lent by the Czech Institute.

Peggy always tells the story of how, as usual, I was slightly overwrought at the dress rehearsal, and my frenzied directions to the chorus led to near disaster. Although I have been speaking English for over thirty years, in moments of excitement I still cannot distinguish between the short sound of 'u' and 'a'. It happened that the chorus in the drinking scene had cups in their hands and caps on their heads. The men of the chorus were singing away, but standing like blocks of wood. 'How many times have you been told to throw up your cups!' I yelled at them.

'Throw up your cups!' Obediently sixteen pewter mugs were thrown up, and fell on the stage with a crash.

They were good old days in the Rosa, and in those times there was hardly an established singer or operatic conductor who hadn't, at one time or another, worked for the company. It was hard work, and we hardly ever saw our homes. During the last year I was with them I was demobilized, naturalized and married, but still the weekly, or fortnightly, round went on, an average of four or five performances a week—you can imagine what some of the wartime hotels and theatrical digs were like. I forgot to say that for over a year I conducted in uniform and whenever the police came round the theatre, as they often did on routine inspections, I dreaded the moment when they would ask me for my papers, because although I had permission of absence from the army I had no work permit, so it was quite a relief when I was finally demobilized. I had never worked with a touring company before, and on the whole it was great fun; there was a spirit of camaraderie among the artists that seems to be missing today. There were always different guest singers to steer through the various productions and, above all, always a Phillips scandal of the moment to talk over. This one was IN, that one was OUT, the new policy was such-and-such, or so-and-so was getting the sack.

Yes, they were good old days, and we were maintaining the fine tradition of the Carl Rosa Company which had run for over sixty years.

I, personally, was greatly encouraged by the response of the public and press all over the country, as shown in the following notices:

Orchestra: new life

When Madame Butterfly made her annual appearance at the Theatre Royal last night there was ample opportunity to delve deep into this remarkable score. For Vilem Tausky has put new life into the Carl Rosa Orchestra, which seemed to have been too sadly neglected in the past. *Birmingham Post*

Carl Rosa Conductor's success

Last night's production had evidently been prepared with particular care, and there was a conductor, Vilem Tausky, to whom the performance owed a great deal. He controlled the orchestra so well that the vocal conversations in *La Traviata* were able to take on at appropriate times an intimacy that would have been a normal effect in the play, but was refreshingly new in grand opera. *Glasgow Herald*

A wonderful performance of Faust

With Joan Hammond in the important role of Marguerite, and the orchestra and chorus under the unobtrusive, but firm guidance of Vilem Tausky the whole opera attained a high level of performance which was a pleasure both to hear and to watch.

Coventry Herald

Unfortunately, this happy state of affairs was not to continue. The public appetite for opera strangely decreased as the memories of opera heard in Italy receded, while in Britain there was little operatic tradition for the new generation to follow. Also the cost of production rose, so that no opera company could run at a profit without subsidy, and Mrs Phillips was unwilling at first to face this fact. Towards the end of my second year with the company, Mr Phillips, who was approaching eighty, contracted pneumonia. At last his wife's oft repeated words, 'He's not fit to do the travelling, you know,' were really true. And so Mrs Phillips gained the titles she had so long coveted, 'General Administrator and Artistic Director', and a bad day for her and for the Rosa it was. She was a gifted woman, but she lacked three essential qualities which her husband possessed, namely sound financial judgement, a certain objectivity in making artistic decisions, and tact in dealing with people both inside and outside the company.

She decided to act immediately in recalling Arthur Hammond, a conductor who had worked with the company before the war, and was a great favourite of hers. She had consistently worked for his re-engagement, which Mr Phillips had adamantly opposed.

I had been asked by the Grand Opera Society of Dublin to conduct some opera during our Christmas break, and I had accepted. It was a position which had formerly been filled by Arthur Hammond. When Mrs Phillips heard of this she wrote me a letter saying she was unable to re-engage me in January, as there were to be drastic cuts in the company and, instead of a musical director, there would be now two conductors. Mrs Phillips added that she would be glad if I would conduct the scheduled performances of *The Kiss* in the coming season, and this I did (I couldn't afford not to), and so ended my days with the Rosa.

10 Freelance, of necessity

At the end of the war I had expected to find it difficult to begin a professional career in Britain, and yet, somehow, the path had been wonderfully smoothed for me. It was the period from 1949 to 1950 which I found very hard indeed. I have said little of my private life up to this time, for while I was in the Army, and later travelling with the Rosa I was hardly ever free to have one. In the last months of 1947, while still with the Rosa, I increased my responsibilities not only with a wife, but also with a mother-in-law and two young step-sons. I gained of course, by having a home of my own for the first time for years, but within a year of my marriage I was finding it difficult to support the household.

We probably felt less deprived than we should have at another time, for in these post-war years so many people were trying to build a new life. Food was still rationed, but what was available we certainly could afford to buy. Clothing was obtainable only with coupons. The shops were still short of many commodities, what goods were available were of a utilitarian standard. When we desperately needed money for extras, we sold things like lace tablecloths, silver goods and parts of my stamp collection, and people gave a good price, because such things were in short supply.

At that time my only secure engagement was a twice yearly season with the Dublin Grand Opera Society, which meant at most a living wage for two months of the year. However, the work was extremely rewarding, for the standard of the society was very high, and it was valuable to me to work with singers of international standing. Another benefit was to work in a country which had not suffered the effects of six years' war. Ireland, always rich in wit and intellect, was an immensely stimulating country to work in at that time. The atmosphere was socially gay, there was almost always a party after the performance, and for me it was like a return to pre-war days. Many of the artists I worked with in Dublin I was to meet again at Covent Garden and Sadler's Wells—Kenneth Neate, Browenstejn, Vroons, James Johnson, Doris Dorée, and Patricia Black, Dublin's leading contralto, with whom I had already worked in the Rosa.

Kenneth Neate had introduced me in London to a very distinguished Irish singer, now retired, Margaret Sheridan, who in her time had sung Madame Butterfly and Mimi in royal performances at Covent Garden. Now I met her again in Dublin, and she told me the tragic story of her career. She was discovered by Marconi, singing for the nuns in an Irish convent. He arranged for her to study in Italy, and there she almost immediately rose to fame, making her début as Mimi, at La Scala in 1919. She sang under Bellezza and Toscanini, and studied *Madame Butterfly* with Puccini himself. She also sang the world première of Mascagni's *Iris*.

La Sheridan, as she was known, was a very natural and intuitive singer, but she had little idea of how, in maturity, technique can help the voice, and she never acquired this very necessary knowledge. One night she was singing Mimi at La Scala when suddenly her voice cracked. She found herself without the art of remedying this, if it should recur, and this created such a psychological panic in her that she never sang in opera again. Whenever she attempted to sing, after a minute or two her throat closed, and she could not go on. HMV Gramophone Company thought that the situation of recording, where she could stop if necessary, might help her, and suggested that she should record some Irish songs with piano. They felt if anyone could give her confidence I could. So we tried two or three times, but although we were alone in the studio it was always the same, a minute or two of the most glorious sound, and then she was unable to go on. She was a beautiful woman, and a charming personality. Later she went to teach and give master classes in New York, but returned to Dublin where she died in 1958.

While I was in Dublin I met Fachtna O'Hanrahain, head of music of Radio Eireann, and he engaged me to give some symphony concerts with the radio orchestra, including the first performance of an overture by the Irish composer Gerard Victory, and the first performance of Martinů's Violin Concerto, played by the Czech violinist, Vaněcek, who was professor of violin at the Royal Irish Academy of Music.

Bruce Dargavel, who sang King Phillip in *Don Carlos*, and Escamillo in Dublin, introduced me to his cousin, Ivor Dargavel, who ran a concert agency in Wales. Ivor was in close touch with Ben Endler, a wealthy industrialist, who had some excess profits which he was anxious to invest in the cause of opera for South Wales. Endler's wife, Elsie Boardman, had been a mezzo soprano in the British National Opera Company under Sir Thomas Beecham, and through Ivor Dargavel they invited me to conduct a week's opera season in Briton Ferry. This I did about twice a year from 1952 to 1954, and I must say that they engaged some of the most distinguished artists available in the United Kingdom at that time, including Geraint Evans, Gwen Catley, Rowland Jones, Patricia Black and Victoria Elliott.

The Welsh went absolutely mad about these opera seasons, and they were some of the most appreciative audiences I have ever played to. I think part of the success of the whole project was because we were able to use their splendid choral societies in *Carmen*, *Rigoletto*, *Il Trovatore* and other operas with chorus. They worked for weeks beforehand and of course it gave our audiences an added interest in the performances. Their enjoyment and enthusiasm built up an atmosphere that I can never forget, and their way of expressing it was typical of their warm Welsh hearts. On one last night the local children presented the principals with armfuls of bluebells and bracken, which they had picked from the hillside that afternoon. The orchestra presented me with a whole side of Welsh bacon, a very welcome tribute in those days of rationing. The last gift was perhaps the most impressive of all. When the performance was over, the chorus, who had worked all day in the steel works, and sung every evening of the week in the opera, lined the galleries around the stage, and sang for me in Welsh with heart and soul. It was their way of saying a final thank you.

Although the Welsh are so gifted chorally, they have little appreciation of orchestral accompaniment; to them the voice is all. During the last few years I have made it my mission, both at National Eisteddfods and at summer schools for orchestral players held in Wales, to make this musical nation realize the role of orchestral accompaniment in opera. I have said, in my halting Welsh, from more than one platform, 'Bread is good, but there are times when it is better with butter on it'.

I remember a little story to illustrate this. It is generally considered to be the right of the chorus master, who has done all the donkey work of the preliminary rehearsals, to conduct a performance, should he so wish. On one occasion, in a little town in a mining valley, I saw to my amazement that the excellent chorus master was about to conduct *Rigoletto* from a tonic sol fa score!

In between opera in Ireland and Wales I was trying to add to my income by doing some arrangements for music publishers and by coaching singers. I even remember on one occasion that I had to wait for a singer to pay his fees in order to have enough money for the fare to get to Wales for one of the opera seasons. But although we were very hard up, they were by no means unhappy days. For one thing it was the first time for ten years that I had really lived at home. Peggy and I had great faith that eventually there would be a breakthrough, and when the exchequer was increased by twenty, fifteen or even five pounds, what a thrill it was!

Somehow there always was plenty to do. We had a comfortable house in Ealing, and I busied myself with redecorating and modernizing it as far as our money allowed. We worked hard at getting the garden in order. The sun seemed to shine oftener in those days, we had many summer meals outside, and I had a little summer-house like Janáček where I used to write music. We did not make a misery of poverty, but were happy to be a family together, and we never gave up entertaining our friends, even if we could only offer them beer, gulyas and sausages. Peggy, who had her invalid mother and two schoolboy sons to look after, could not work away from home, but she began to use her Froebel training to specialize in remedial work for children with reading and writing difficulties. It was an advantage that the pupils came to the house, and the money she earned helped our finances to a considerable extent.

The Irish opera season finished about 22 December and I used to return from Dublin like Father Christmas, laden with turkey, ham, biscuits, chocolate, all the things that were still rationed in England. I also had money in my pocket, and there used to be a two-day spending spree, buying all the Christmas presents for which there had been no money until my return. In the end, when the breakthrough finally came, it was as an indirect result of my applying for a post against my better judgement. The BBC were advertising for a conductor for the newly formed West of England Orchestra, based in Bristol, a post for which I had every qualification, and a few to spare. I decided I really couldn't afford not to apply. I was shortlisted, interviewed and the post went to another applicant. Two or three days later Kenneth Wright, artists' manager of the BBC, phoned me on his own behalf and that of Steuart Wilson, head of music in London, both of whom had been on the board at that interview, and had apparently disagreed with the decision then taken.

'Would you like to go to the BBC in Belfast for three months and build up our library there, and we'd also like you to undertake some orchestral arrangements of Irish tunes? And in the meantime,' said Kenneth Wright, 'because it will take a little time to get these arrangements made, would you like to orchestrate my "Tobacco Suite" for me?'

That was the moment when my fortune changed. I shall always remember that the same day he rang Peggy and said, 'Tell Vilem not buy any manuscript paper, I am sending some over.' It showed a thoughtfulness and a kindness I shall never forget.

On the first of November 1949, I started to work in the Belfast library, where they promptly christened me Terence O'Tausky.

I arranged many traditional Irish tunes for the orchestra, including 'Buttermilk Loney', which still pays dividends through the Performing Right Society. For many years my returns showed a constant repetition of an item listed as 'Harken, my good sirs. 6/8d'. Although glad of every 6/8d I couldn't imagine what I had written with that title. Eventually it dawned on me that the money came regularly around December. This was the English translation of a Czech carol I had arranged, and which hit the jackpot every Christmas. Towards the end of my contract, David Curry, the conductor of the Belfast Orchestra, fell ill, and I took his place for three months. By the time he was ready for work again the same situation had arisen in Glasgow. Kemlo Stevens, their conductor, was ill, and the BBC asked me to transfer to Glasgow where I took his place for another three months. By this time we were well into 1950, and before I left Glasgow I had an offer from the BBC Variety Orchestra in Manchester to conduct two shows a week there.

With the prospect of an income of £1,500 a year and some expenses, our financial situation began to improve, and after nearly a year in Belfast and Glasgow I was able to live at home again, although of course I had to travel constantly between London and Manchester. My new post might not initially have seemed likely to stretch my professional capabilities fully, but it was in fact far more of a test of musicianship than one would imagine, and also the greatest fun.

Playing for variety artists demands far more flexibility in a conductor than symphonic conducting, where the conductor's interpretation is the ruling factor. It has more in common with operatic work, where the conductor is serving the individual artist as well as keeping the music going. In opera every performance is individual, and depends on the conductor being aware of the particular needs of the cast for that performance. 'Is the prima donna in good voice tonight? How long will she want to hold that top C? . . . The tenor is beginning a cold, and I shall have to help him to save his voice for the aria in the last act . . . Is the baritone going to miss the same two bars as he did last time, and if so how am I going to get the chorus entrance right?' Such are the questions that occupy the mind of the conductor during the opera. The same kind of awareness is needed in variety, for the comedians are always 'feeling for the house', and one can never be sure that one will be playing the music as it lies on the desk. The artist may decide to add an extra chorus, to put in a gag that has just occurred to him, or to leave out a piece of patter; the conductor cannot relax for a moment.

I shall never regret the days of conducting for variety in Manchester, for the Hulme Hippodrome where we recorded the BBC radio shows on Sundays was the home of really great variety. To begin with, the Northern Variety Orchestra were a great bunch of characters, especially Ken Frith, our brilliant pianist, whom we nicknamed the Problem Child. He was devoted to an eccentric and undependable vintage Bentley, and I never knew whether he would arrive in time for the performance, but when he made it his playing held exactly the improvizational character that variety needs. I am very proud when I think of the artists who worked with me, some of them beginning their careers at the Hippodrome. Benny Hill, then a milkman, Frankie Howerd and Al Read, all just beginning to make their names. Morecambe and Wise appeared often in our programmes, and Elsie and Doris Waters too. I remember Tessie O'Shea as a very dominant lady who, like Chaliapin, tried to beat out the time for me. So I said, handing her the baton, 'Right, Tessie, you conduct and I'll sing!' and we ended up in helpless laughter.

Once, when I was conducting *The Flying Dutchman* in Nottingham, my old compatriot, Vic Oliver (son-in-law of Winston Churchill, and born a Czech), was playing variety at the Empire and our stage doors backed on to each other. He called me 'the Flying Dutchman' for ever more, because he said wherever he went I turned up in one capacity or another.

Another very great artist I worked with was Gracie Fields. She had a magnificent voice which would have served her well had she not preferred to use it for comedy, 'mooking abaht' with it, and who is to say she chose wrongly, for she gave pleasure to millions? She had that great art which can turn laughter to tears in the twinkling of an eye. One night she came on stage and pretended to be surprised to find me as conductor. 'Why it's our Vilem! Ooh, I do loove you, give us a kiss loove, and let's hope your wife's listening.' She was.

And last but not least, Jimmy Edwards. When he got going on that trombone, I couldn't trust myself to look, for I couldn't have gone on conducting. We took two young boys to see him at the Palladium one night, and when, afterwards, we went round to his dressing room, Peggy made some crack about the performance. He fixed her with a steely eye. 'Hi,' he said, 'Jim does the funnies!'

Just as at the turn of the twentieth century music hall reached the height of its popularity, so now some of these great artists I worked with were enjoying the heyday of radio variety, later on to be succeeded in its own turn by television shows. As a last tribute I must add that I shall always connect my long and happy association in *Variety Fanfare* with the two northern BBC producers, Alec Hayes and Ronnie Taylor, who wrote our scripts.

This excursion into more frivolous entertainment never affected the opportunities given me to conduct in other fields, and there was one occasion when the *Radio Times* billed a recording of the Al Read show on the Light Programme at 8 pm from the Hippodrome in Manchester, while on the Home Service at the same hour there was a live broadcast of Richard Strauss' *Salome* from Covent Garden. I was the conductor in both cases.

I can remember only one exception to the general rule that nothing I promote for myself is ever really successful. After I had been working for a year or so in the BBC Manchester, I plucked up courage to go to Maurice Johnstone, the head of music, and ask him if I might at some time conduct the BBC Northern Orchestra. Maurice was not only a very knowledgeable musician, but also a very sympathetic character. 'Of course,' he said, 'why not? I heard you conduct *Tosca* here at the Opera House and was most impressed.'

And so began a series of concerts in which I tried to offer lesser known works, and first performances of British works. Gordon Thorne, who succeeded Maurice as head of music, told me that Maurice said to him, 'I thought I had a pretty wide repertoire, but this chap keeps offering me composers and works I've never heard of'.

It was a great pleasure to work for Maurice Johnstone; he had a sense of adventure in music and great enthusiasm for a good programme. Gradually I did more and more work with the symphony orchestra, of which John Hopkins was the principal conductor, and a year later I became associate conductor. Memorable occasions included conducting the first two symphonies by Bruckner, at that time a composer rarely played in Britain. To commemorate the fiftieth anniversary of Dvořáks' death, I conducted the whole cycle of his nine symphonies, including the recently discovered Number One (*Zlonické Zvony*).

During this time there was a heated altercation in the national press about the great difficulty contemporary British composers had in obtaining a hearing of new works. I was able to write to the *Daily Telegraph*, claiming, on behalf of the BBC Northern Orchestra, that no fewer than twenty-five first perfromances of new works had been given during the year. I continued to work with the Northern Orchestra until I took up my appointment with the BBC Concert Orchestra in London in 1956.

Now the hard times were over, and work started to pour in, although financially it took us a long time to catch up on those two lean years of 1949 and 1950. In the years between 1951 and 1953, some important doors began to open for me, all in the field of opera. The first was when Joan Cross and Anne Wood asked me to work for them at the National School of Opera which they founded to train young opera singers. I worked there from the earliest demonstration class, held at the end of the first year's work in 1952, until their final brilliant production of Auber's *Fra Diavolo* in 1967.

These two redoubtable ladies of widely differing gifts and character made an excellent teaching combination. Joan already had a distinguished career behind her as a principal soprano, and later would become the director of Sadler's Wells. She had tremendous theatrical flair as a producer and was a good judge of voices, but was so sharply critical that many of the singers were terrified of her tongue. But she could be kind and encouraging as well, and if the spark was there in a pupil, Joan was very clever at teaching the necessary technique. Anne, in contrast, seemed quiet and gentle. She had an excellent talent for organization, and was gifted in dealing with people. She had been a singer herself, and was a great purist where the art of singing was concerned, and, in matters of taste, whether musical or theatrical, she was implacable. One tended to think on first acquaintance that the more flamboyant Joan was the dominant partner. Joan and I were often ready to accept slight imperfections for the sake of the overall effect in performance, not so Anne who looked at matters differently. When I had known them only a short time I was surprised, when Joan and I agreed over some small matter of direction, to hear her say, 'I don't think we shall carry Anne with us, you know how obstinate she is'. I soon learned that each had sometimes to bow to the other. Ava June, Marie Collier, Inia Te Wiata, Johanna Peters, Myer Fredman (the conductor), April Cantelo, Kenneth Sandford (of D'Oyly Carte fame) and Rae Woodland are among the artists who can be grateful for their training at that school.

In 1967 the Arts Council proposed to incorporate the National School of Opera in the London Opera Centre. Joan and Anne were asked to remain on the staff, but with Dr Procter Gregg as director. Unfortunately, differences of opinion arose and, after a lot of newspaper publicity, Joan Cross and Anne Wood resigned. Undaunted they fought on, and from the ashes arose the Phoenix Opera Company which had the special function of helping young people who had recently completed their training, and needed professional operatic experience.

It saddens me that the Phoenix Opera, which won such golden opinions at festivals up and down the country, is now in abeyance. For ten years the company received a grant from the Arts Council, but in 1976 it was refused, nobody seems to know quite why. The company has certain assets, but would be unable to launch a tour without subsidy. Joan Cross by then had retired to Suffolk, Anne Wood still holds the reins as general administrator, and I am still one of the artistic directors.

Now another unexpected opportunity occurred. In September

1951 I had a friendly and informal letter from David Webster of the Royal Opera House, Covent Garden, saying, 'Would you like to conduct *The Queen of Spades* by Tchaikowsky for us at Covent Garden in the coming season? If so, come and see me'.

So, on 14 November 1951 I began my career at Covent Garden by taking over *The Queen of Spades*, conducted in the previous season by Kleiber. Hilda Zadek sang Lisa, Edgar Evans, Hermann, my old friend Kraus sang Tomsky and, needless to say, the orchestra was a joy to handle. Perhaps the outstanding performance was Edith Coates, Harry Powell Lloyd's wife, in the title role; she had made a study of this part that was so imaginative that it can never be forgotten.

In 1952 I conducted *Tosca* with Kinasiewicz in the main role and Otakar Kraus as Scarpia, as we had done together so often at the Rosa. Our Cavaradossi was James Johnston, who had sung with me in Dublin and was now a leading tenor at the Garden. In the following year, I conducted a revival of *The Queen of Spades*, but this time with Ljuba Wellitsch as Lisa. Later that same year I began a series of performances with Gré Brouwenstijn singing Leonora in *Il Trovatore*. *The Times* said of her: 'Miss Brouwenstijn is that rare phenomenon, a Verdi stylist from a non-latin country (Holland). Her voice is of the right weight and colour, she sings with appreciation of Verdi's melodic and dramatic structure'.

The notice concluded: 'Perhaps the most vital feature of the performance was the orchestral playing under Mr Vilem Tausky, who secured buoyantly rhythmical accompaniments and strong climaxes, but still found time to point to Verdi's orchestral detail'.

It is a pity that I can't tell you any intimate, personal stories about the many distinguished artists I worked with at Covent Garden, but this was not like a touring company where one's free time was spent with the singers, nor even like the Welsh and Irish opera seasons. In these post-war years the aim of Covent Garden was to build up a strong company of important British artists. In the meantime the main roles were taken by guest artists from overseas whose names would help to fill the house.

Naturally, they arrived for rehearsal, sang the role and departed. There was not time for a conductor to get to know them on any very personal level. An outstanding example was Kinasiewicz, who arrived at the Opera House at 4 o'clock one afternoon, and, after a private run-through with me, and never having seen our production, did a superb performance of Turandot that evening.

Among British artists who were by now making names in the company of these international singers were Geraint Evans, Monica Sinclair, James Johnston, Blanche Turner, Michael Langdon, William McAlpine and Edgar Evans.

I came to know Christl Goltz from Germany rather better, because, between 1952 and 1954, she sang Strauss' *Salome* with me so many times. She was a delightful, warmhearted woman, and anyone less like the character of Salome it would be difficult to imagine, but although I also conducted for Ljuba Wellitsch and the American Dorothy Dow, in this role, Goltz surpassed them both, in characterization and voice. I was delighted to have this review in *The Times:* 'The chief difference between this and previous performances here reviewed was the conductorship of Mr Vilem Tausky. His control of this performance was sure; the hateful yet fascinating drama progressed fluently, with firm attack, emotional intensity, and diversity of colour.'

In 1954 I greatly enjoyed conducting Verdi's *Masked Ball* on a tour with Joan Sutherland, Edgar Evans, Adèle Leigh, Jess Walters and Geraint Evans. That was a cast to remember, and the shape of things to come!

Of one of these performances a critic said: 'The orchestra again distinguished itself by some splendid playing. In control was Vilem Tausky whose authority and competence are so marked. Few conductors could make more of this opera than he achieved.'

There was one British singer who could not fail to make an impression on fellow artists, even if one worked with her in only one show. I was privileged to work with her in many, over a number of years. Her name was Edith Coates, the wife of Harry Powell Lloyd. I have said before that Harry had a pessimistic nature, and I remember one night as we were coming home on the underground, and talking of certain difficulties to be overcome, Harry said in his gentle way, 'I'm inclined to look on the gloomy side, Edie has rather a *gay* nature'. This was an understatement. Edie was really a bewitching person, in the true sense of that misused word. She had an excellent contralto voice, but above all she could cast a spell to make you believe whatever she wished. This was the product of a lively imagination, and great audience compulsion. Whatever part she took she dominated the stage if it was dramatically right for her to do so. Anyone who saw her play The Queen of Spades, Herodias, or the Witch in Bernard Miles's production of Purcell's *Dido* with Flagstad and Thomas Hemsley in the cast, or heard her sing Ulrica or Azucena will know at once what I mean.

Offstage she was a true 'enfant terrible'. Like most people of lively imagination she was very highly strung and this quality she covered up with inconsequential remarks, delivered with an unforgettable giggle. When the Covent Garden Company were on tour in Leeds, Lord Harewood had been to several performances. One afternoon he invited certain members to come over to Harewood House. He drove over to fetch us in one of his big cars. We all huddled politely and modestly in the back seats. Lord Harewood sat at the wheel and seemed as shy as his guests, nobody knew quite how to get the conversation going. Edie arrived, late and breathless, threw herself into the front seat beside him and opened fire with a hearty, 'How's y' folks?' Everyone laughed and the ice was broken.

I shall end the memories of the Royal Opera House with a personal reminiscence which I know will be shared by all who worked together in those days, and who patronized the Berengaria, the little Italian restaurant round the corner in Long Acre where many of us used to foregather after performances. The proprietor was devoted to opera and to all those who made opera come alive. Presumably he made his living in the earlier part of the day, for, once the opera was over and the artists began to drift in, they took command. Orders flew thick and fast for all and any of the dishes on the rather sketchy post-war menu. Criticisms of performances were hurled from table to table, mezzos sang the tenor parts, sopranos corrected the renderings given by their elders and betters. 'All right, if you can do it better, let's hear you!' was the challenge. Most delightful of all, when closing time drew near, the proprietor passed round a soup plate, each put in what he or she could afford and we all went happily home.

There was once a Welshman called Bill Smith, a most unlikely name for a Welshman you must agree, who loved opera. He also had unlimited enthusiasm and vision. That he knew a good voice when he heard one goes without saying, or he couldn't have been a Welshman. He was a car salesman and owned a big garage from which he had made a good deal of money, always a help when one is trying to realize an ideal. It was Bill Smith who laid the foundations of the Welsh National Opera Company as we know it today.

He began by preparing operas with important chorus parts, and for these he drew on the best amateur choral societies around Swansea and Cardiff, and engaged professional singers, many Welsh ones among them, to sing as principals. He started by preparing for a fortnight's season in each of these major cities, and the evening rehearsals were held in his garage. The successes gained by these seasons led to the formation of a Welsh Opera Company in 1946.

In 1951 Bill asked me to become musical director of the company, and he engaged the Bournemouth Symphony Orchestra for the coming season. Charles Groves, their resident conductor, shared the conducting with me. The standard of the performances rose rapidly, and in 1954 we received an invitation from the directors of Sadler's Wells to give a week's season in their theatre in the following July. It was a great honour for a new company to achieve, and also made for an interesting musical occasion in London, as we presented operas quite unfamiliar to London audiences. Charles Groves conducted Verdi's *Nabucco*, Arwel Hughes conducted his own Welsh folk opera. I was responsible for *Rigoletto* and *The Sicilian Vespers*.

Kenneth Loveland of the South Wales Echo wrote:

The company's triumphant début at Sadler's Wells, when

they packed the theatre night after night with what was virtually an unknown repertoire, caused a complete revision of opinion about opera standards in the provinces; the week at Bournemouth, and then this Cardiff fortnight were a climax to the most inspired burst of activity the company has ever experienced.

The balance of the Company's success is more evenly spread. For this much credit must be given to Vilem Tausky, who, in four seasons has widened the approach of the company . . . The Bartered Bride must now be ranked as one of the finest shows in the repertoire. Vilem Tausky, who indeed, should know all the tricks of Smetana's music, has put the stamp of authority on this production . . . In Cavelleria Rusticana he brings to the score a sense of urgency and passion, and builds up a masterly tension in every big climax.

Both the Swansea and Cardiff seasons were very successful. In Cardiff we played ten operas in thirteen days, to crowded houses. But the great triumph was the season at Sadler's Wells, where, in one of the hottest weeks London has ever known, every performance was packed, and the enthusiasm for the whole project, and perhaps especially for the Welsh singing, was unbounded. As far as I remember it was also the first time that respectable London audiences sat in their shirt sleeves. There really was a very special feeling of excitement about that week, it had all the atmosphere of opera in Italy.

Since those days the fortunes of the Welsh National Opera Company, like those of most opera companies, have risen and fallen throughout the years, but it is thanks to the vision and enthusiasm of Bill Smith that a National Welsh Opera Company has been so firmly established.

I remained musical director until I took over the BBC Concert Orchestra in 1956. During the period of my appointment, I had conducted La Traviata, Rigoletto, Sicilian Vespers, Die Fledermaus, The Bartered Bride, Cavalleria Rusticana and Pagliacci, La Bohème, Tosca and Faust. I loved working with the Welsh. I am a Slav by birth and I find a great affinity between the Celts and the Slavs.

They have the same natural, uninhibited emotions, they are not over-civilized, and they have beautiful voices. If you listen to the Don Cossack Choir and then to a good Welsh male voice choir you will feel the same emotional pulse and vibration in each.

In July 1953 I received a summons from Norman Tucker at Sadler's Wells: 'We are doing *Hansel and Gretel* for Christmas, Harry Powell Lloyd is producing for us, would you like to conduct?'

I was delighted at the invitation for I admired the administration of Sadler's Wells at that time, and enjoyed the prospect of working for an audience which included a complete cross section of the society. I loved Humperdinck's music, an ideal choice for a Christmas production. Harry made a truly magic forest, with owl's eyes which suddenly lit up among the trees and the loveliest gingerbread house you ever saw. The dream pantomime angels were, as they should be, quite out of this world.

We were extremely fortunate to have Marion Studholme as Gretel. She looked like a real little German girl, not like an operatic actress dressed as one, and yet her voice had the weight so necessary to carry over Humperdinck's orchestration which is very heavy in places. Hansel was one of Anna Pollak's best roles. When one remembers her triumphant Orloffsky in *Die Fledermaus*, and her performance as the kitchen boy in *Rusalka*, one might be tempted to think her talent lay in 'Hosenrollen'. But remember, too, she was equally successful as Carmen, as Lady Nelson (Lennox Berkeley) and as the secretary in Menotti's *The Consul* and one realizes that Anna Pollak was an extremely good operatic actress over a very wide field of rôles. She was a popular member of the company, a very original character, and a real trouper to work with. We were all glad when, after twenty years work at Sadler's Wells, she received an OBE for her services to music.

Before the rehearsals for *Hansel and Gretel* were completed, Norman Tucker had asked me if I would prepare and conduct *The Pearl Fishers* by Bizet. This was an almost unknown opera in Britain and had been newly translated for the occasion. The sets by John Piper and the production by Basil Coleman gave it great distinction.

Thus began a long and happy association with Sadler's Wells, where I conducted both new and repertoire operas, and, as this work covered a number of years, I shall mention the more important occasions as we come to them.

11 Ten years with the B.B.C. Concert Orchestra

In the years 1954–6 I became more and more involved with programmes for the BBC Northern Orchestra, while my work with the Northern Variety Orchestra was gradually taken over by Alyn Ainsworth. He began as an arranger and conductor for the BBC. Later he formed the BBC dance band in Manchester and has now a top backing band which is used for both radio and television.

I seemed to be constantly on the train between Manchester and London where I was doing a great deal of work at Covent Garden and also working each week at the National School of Opera. Sir John Barbirolli was also conducting at Covent Garden, and returning to Manchester to conduct the Hallé. I remember we had two good friends in the booking office at Manchester station, who called us, 'The ships that pass in the night'. They always saw to it that I had compartment 7 or 8, which are not over the wheels, and when there was no sleeper available they provided blankets and pillows in a first class compartment. Such friends can do a great deal to ensure that a busy musician arrives at his work on form, and I have reason to be grateful to many who, in different ways, have made conditions easier for me. I remember on one occasion when I travelled from Manchester to Dartington over night and conducted an opera before returning to London where I was conducting at the Garden—all in the space of forty-eight hours. When I arrived at Dartington at 6 am Anne Wood had got up to cook a hot breakfast for me. I don't know what we musicians would do without a few people like that around.

In 1954 I began my association with the English Opera Group which had been formed by Benjamin Britten and Peter Pears, and I was asked to prepare that year's operatic programme for the Aldeburgh Festival. It was to be a new one-act opera, *The Dinner Engagement* by Lennox Berkeley, preceded by an eighteenth-century opera by Arne, made into one act and re-orchestrated by Arthur Oldham. *Dinner Engagement* was an enchanting piece with a very witty and tender libretto by Paul Dehn. It was well produced by William Chappell with a distinguished cast of April Cantelo, Alexander Young, Emilie Hooke, James Sharp, Flora Nielsen and Catherine Wilson. Of course Berkeley's outstanding sense of style brought to life both the romance and the humour in this sophisticated little opera. Arne's *Love in a Village* made an excellent piece to team with it as it had the same kind of sophistication and style, but was set in eighteenth-century rural England.

The Aldeburgh festival was then in its early days and the ill-fated Snape, let alone The Maltings, had not yet been envisaged. The operas and all the main musical events were then held in the little Memorial Hall, but, because Britten and Pears were the moving spirits behind the festival, all the musical world and a great deal of social London flocked to Aldeburgh, rather as they flock to Glyndebourne, and it was amusing to see them all adjusting to their much less sophisticated surroundings.

Let me first say that the comments I am going to make about the Aldeburgh set-up have nothing at all to do with Britten and Pears who were only concerned with giving people the best artists and performances that could be secured. Nevertheless, they were surrounded by admirers intent on creating an intellectual and social mystique around the festival and emphasizing to the visitors the subtle social hierarchy of it. The place to stay was the Wentworth Hotel, and here the Royal Family, as we called them (Peter, Ben and Joan Cross), did their entertaining. Next in order was the Brudenell, where we stayed, followed by the Copper Kettle and various local inns. Of course it was also very *comme il faut* to stay outside Aldeburgh with friends who motored one in. As well as the chief musical events, which were all first class, there were other festival happenings which the visitors gained kudos from attending, a lecture on bird-song by Ludwig Koch at 11 am or Czech folksongs conducted by Imogen Holst, and perhaps the rarest flight of fancy of all, I remember 'lute songs by moonlight' by Arda Mandikian, which took place after the performance of the evening's opera. It would have been easy to have taken this all too seriously.

I remember we were invited for lunch at the Wentworth by Britten and Pears one Saturday. It was the last day of the festival and our fellow guests were in immaculate morning dress, with white rosebuds in their buttonholes. They were the soloists in the St. Matthew Passion, to be sung later in the parish church. It was an afternoon of glorious sunshine. I kept very quiet through lunch and, when we had taken our leave, I said to Peggy, 'I've had a gruelling week, I'm not going to the Matthew Passion, I'm going to turn up my trousers and paddle.' And I did, in front of the sacred Wentworth, secure in the knowledge that they were all sweating it out in the parish church.

In 1955 I was invited by Maurice Johnstone, who by this time was head of music in London, to conduct the BBC Symphony Orchestra in all six of Martinů's symphonies, in honour of his sixtieth birthday. This gave me great pleasure as I had been in constant contact with him between the years 1932–40, and I recognized in him the natural successor to Dvořák and Janáček.

I first met him during rehearsals for his ballet *Špaliček* when it was being produced at Brno in 1932. I was the solo pianist. At that time he was just beginning to win some kind of recognition, and his work in Paris, where he had lived for the last eight years, was punctuated by visits to Prague and Brno to supervise the premières of his operas and ballets. The first performance of his opera *The Three Marias* was given at the Opera House in Brno, and I was in charge of the preparations.

At that time Martinů was forty-four years old, but he looked much younger. He was tall and wiry with a very quiet manner, but was capable of getting into a royal rage if his ideas of production were not realized and faithfully carried out.

I saw him next in 1939 in that French country house which was for the use of Czech artists as he often came to visit us there. Sad as he was, and full of apprehension for his homeland, he was also full of hope for the future, and The Double Concerto, which he wrote at this period, contains some of his best music, courageous and positive in character.

My last glimpse of Martinů must have been just before the fall of France. He was blacklisted by the Nazis and had to leave Paris. He and his wife, carrying only a small suitcase, set out for southern France—further destination unknown—leaving behind them irreplaceable scores and manuscripts. By this time I was in the Czech Army outside Paris, and in his flight Martinů paused to see his friends. Of course he was only one of many creative artists undergoing the same loss of all that they held precious, but, because he was especially helpless in everyday life, it was very sad to see him in this state. He thought and spoke continually of those in Czechoslovakia. 'They are thinking of us at home, counting on us—and we cannot and must not disappoint them,' he said.

I have always thought that his earlier background helped to determine the essential character of his music. Martinů was born in 1890 in a tower; a fact of greater importance than might appear at first sight. His parents were caretakers of the tower of a country church in Polička, a little town on Moravia's borders, and Martinů spent the first thirteen years of his life two hundred dark, winding steps above the rest of the world. It was from this isolated vantage that he first observed the rich pattern of Czech country life. In these early days he absorbed the knowledge of folk music which has been one of the strongest interests of his life, and a dominant factor in his music. From the parapet of the tower, every day of the week, he was able to watch processions of funerals, weddings and other Czech festivities. On Sundays, organ music and the singing of churchgoers filled his ears, and on Sundays and weekdays alike the passing of time was marked by the ceaseless ticking of the tower clock.

But, although he lived in a tower, it was no ivory one, and Martinů never wanted it to be. His whole musical life was directed towards the means of making his music comprehensible to all. 'My deepest conviction is the essential nobility of thoughts and things which are quite simple.'

Martinů had always known what he wanted to say in music. His difficulty was in finding some one from whom he could learn how to say it. Roussel and his circle solved his problem by showing him how to combine the national element in his music with modern French technique. One day, while examining a work by Roussel, he realized that he must go and live in Paris. He went to Paris for a few months, and stayed for seventeen years, only leaving when forced to flee during German occupation.

Through Koussevitsky, the American conductor, Martinů's music had become quite well-known in America, and when he was obliged to leave France in 1940, it was natural that he should try to carry on his career in the New World, where a great deal of his best music was written. In 1952 he returned to France.

In 1955 I was delighted to renew the old contact with him and wrote to him in Nice to let him know that within the next few weeks all his six symphonies would be played and broadcast.

BBC TV interviewed me on the programme *Monitor* to celebrate this event, and began their interview by showing the facsimile of a letter to me from Martinů in which he wrote, in his halting English, his ideas about England in a message to the BBC.

Here goes. In the beginning of things England was for me only a colour in the geographic map. France was red, England was yellow. Later on I learnt that Handel came there, Berlioz came and Dvořák came. And they liked him and his music. I thought: 'England, England, very far from my little village on the border of Moravia! They like Dvořák over there, may be, one day they will like my music too! Youngster's dreams. There was not yet a radio at this time and I didn't have the scores, except in my head. And the years went on, the world changed in an unexpected way. Half of my dreams became true, my music shall be performed in England. If they like it over there the second half of my dream shall become true too. This of course, I do not know, I am only hoping it shall. The scores, I have many of them now, might be some of them will evoke the old memories of Dvořák in a new version. It could seem that this music has not so much in common with him but it does.

Bohuslav Martinů

This cycle was very successful. Since those days Martinů's work has become much more popular with the British public, and he has even featured as the composer of the week on radio.

In the summer of 1955 my old friend Barbirolli fell ill, and I conducted a Viennese Promenade Concert with the Hallé in his place, at the Albert Hall. He sent me a typical Barbirolli telegram, reading, 'Thank you, dear colleague, thank you'.

It was a pouring wet Saturday night, and when Edgar Mais, that well-known factotum of the Symphony Orchestra, came and warned me in his solemn way, 'They've got the streamers out, maestro,' in my overwrought state I imagined he must be referring to getting the drenched queues under cover. When I got on to the rostrum I soon found out what the streamers were!

One day in the summer of 1956, while I was working in the BBC office in Manchester, there was a discussion going on as to what reshuffle there was likely to be among BBC music staff, as Charles Mackerras was leaving the Concert Orchestra.

'Who do you think will get it?'

'Oh, so and so, or so and so,' went the gossip.

'Nobody asked me if I would like it,' I said quietly.

Gordon Thorne stared at me in surprise. 'Your name was mentioned,' he said, 'but I told them that I didn't think you would be interested.'

'On the contrary, I am,' I replied.

Within a day or two he had arranged an interview for me with Frank Wade, the head of light music in London. The post had two obvious advantages for me. It based me in London, where most of my other work lay, and for the first time for many years I would be directing my own orchestra. After my interview with Frank Wade I knew beyond all doubt this was the man I wanted to work for, for he had the same views about music as I had; he had great aims for the orchestra and unbounded administrative skill and enthusiasm to help him carry them out. In October 1956 I

123

was appointed conductor of the BBC Concert Orchestra, a post I was to hold for a decade. The qualities I saw in Frank caused me to dedicate to him the march 'Men of Tomorrow', which I wrote for the Concert Orchestra in 1958. Here is the way in which he thought of the orchestra and its function: 'The BBC Concert Orchestra, with its conductor Vilem Tausky, plays to capacity audiences both in London concert halls and in the large cities outside. Its programmes, designed to satisfy widely ranging tastes contain an infinite variety. Its regular broadcasts are listened to by anything from one to two million people. It is a full orchestra of 55 players, a virtuoso ensemble belonging to the whole community. Its versatility leads it from Sullivan and Strauss to the belief that parts of Stravinsky's *Firebird* ballet have immediate appeal and can be regarded as light music.'

I myself wrote about the orchestra in an article for the Light Music Festival of 1958:

The BBC Concert Orchestra has a unique position in the entertainment world today and it tries to serve the needs of the British public. In truly British tradition, it has evolved, one would say, rather than been formed. It arose in answer to the need for a certain repertoire of music that was missing from musical programmes in this country.

One of the functions of music is to entertain, and we are not ashamed of the fact that our programmes are built from music that is primarily for your enjoyment—everything from Mozart to Gershwin is included.

We refuse to allow you to be frightened of the great composers, and will prove to you that Handel, Mozart, Elgar and Stravinsky also wrote music which everyone can enjoy and understand. Do not think that the artificial barrier which is so often made between light and serious music was recognized by the composers themselves. Sometimes they wrote to earn bread and butter and sometimes urged by their genius. Fortunately inspiration is not so tidily arranged that the good music was that which they wrote of their own volition and the bad music written for money. It has always seemed to me a good thing that a composer should have to earn his living, because it keeps him in touch with the tastes of the people, and to write for their needs is one of the justifications of his existence.

Mozart himself wrote much of his greatest music to settle his debts. People nowadays regard him as a highbrow composer and yet he wrote some of the dance music of his day and never hesitated to include an errand boy's whistle or a popular folksong in his compositions.

Perhaps it seems a long cry from Mozart to Gershwin, but Gershwin too wrote music for the people in their own idiom, and much of it was music of inspiration. Therefore we find nothing strange in including music by both these composers in our programmes. My main concern is that the music we play shall always be good in its own right.

You would be wrong to imagine that when we play 'popular music' we are in any sense playing down to our public. All of us enjoy occasionally to hear music which relaxes, or diverts us, or even makes us feel pleasantly sentimental, and I say we are musical snobs when we don't admit it.

This brings me to the instrument, which provides it—the BBC Concert Orchestra. It is a full orchestra of wide experience and high technical ability. This is essential because of the wide range of music in many different styles which we play.

I shall not attempt to fill in details of the ten fulfilling years I spent with the orchestra, but I must tell you of a few of the highlights we shared. I made my début with a series of broadcasts introduced by Marjorie Westbury and produced by Neil Sutherland entitled 'All the best'.

Then Frank Wade promoted an entirely new idea, which was that the public should get to know the principals of the orchestra through an introduction in words by the conductor, followed by a solo from the principal concerned. This was an immensely popular series entitled *At Home* and we ran the gamut of principals from the leader to the percussion. This series lasted for two years, and as far as possible I arranged that the soloists chose their own pieces. These programmes made for rapport between the orchestra and the listeners, and meant that when we appeared at the seaside, or in industrial towns, we had a ready-made audience, eager to see people they had already made friends with on the air.

The peak of the year was reached for the Concert Orchestra in the Light Music Festival, held annually at the Festival Hall, which has now been running for over twenty years. Frank Wade was at pains to see that the orchestra was at the top of its form as June came round each year. He also commissioned new works to be played in the festival from important composers such as Malcolm Williamson, Iain Hamilton, Elizabeth Lutyens, Malcolm Arnold, Phyllis Tate, Gordon Jacob and Eric Coates. Concerts were held on five consecutive Saturdays and Frank arranged that each year they should have a dominant theme. The year that I perhaps remember most clearly was one when each concert featured the music of a European country, and included a visiting conductor from Germany, France, Denmark, Switzerland and Austria. Each foreign conductor was featured during the concert in music from his own country, and at each concert the ambassador from that country was present. This of course interested the featured countries in the work of the BBC Concert Orchestra, and although it was too expensive to transport the orchestra, it resulted in several exchange engagements for its conductor. I was invited to appear in Paris, Copenhagen, Vienna, Oslo and Hamburg, and was able to present some of the works by British composers which had been written for the Concert Orchestra.

These engagements led to invitations to conduct in other Continental countries. While I was in Denmark I went on to Norway conducting in both Oslo and Bergen. Here Peggy and I had the pleasure of being entertained by the well known Norwegian composer, Harold Saeverud, in his unique and charming home, built entirely of local stone and stripped pinewood. I shall never forget, either, the enchantment of a sparkling sunlit January morning when Edvard Grieg's home was opened specially for us by his biographer. Time rolled back, and as the poet told of the fiery little composer and his adored wife, Nina the singer, it seemed that they lived again. They have no graves, but we were shown the cliff facing the lake where in the raw clay is scratched, as with a stick poignantly: EDVARD — NINA.

Down by the lake was his working hut, just as he left it, with a shabby upright piano on which I was invited to play. Close by was a chair with scores on it, for, like Brahms, he was so short that he found difficulty in reaching the keyboard. My mind flew back to Magda Dvořák, who had so often sung with him, and told us many stories about him.

When I went to Finland my visit was made memorable by the kindness and the friendship of the Baroness Kyra van Essen. A great music lover, she solved all problems, and because of the language difficulty I should have found it very difficult to communicate with the Finns if it had not been for her help. In all I went three times to Copenhagen, and one occasion I also had a broadcast in Stockholm where my cousin Rischka Fall lives, the daughter of Leo Fall, and a familiar figure of my early days. We made contact after a gap of thirty years, and I am glad to say I am still in touch with her.

In Hamburg I was asked for two of my own compositions, which had been played in the Light Music Festival, my Harmonica Concerto played by Tommy Reilly, and the orchestral suite 'From our Village'. I also conducted at the Munich Festival where Owen Brannigan and April Cantelo sang excerpts from *Our Man in Havana* by Malcolm Williamson.

To my astonishment I was asked to do Gilbert and Sullivan for a radio performance in Copenhagen. Nothing daunted, I set off, but I couldn't imagine how Gilbert, so typically English and idiomatic in a dated way, would translate into Danish. In the event however, it must have been an excellent translation, because I was able to set just the tempi I needed. They gave me very good singers, with a great sense of humour. We did *Trial by Jury* on a Sunday afternoon to an invited audience, who loved it, and the next year I was asked back to do *HMS Pinafore* which was equally successful. Another time I was invited to conduct a concert of British light music on the occasion of the opening of the Tivoli Gardens.

Looking back on the early years with the Concert Orchestra I am surprised that somehow this was a period of great creative activity for me, as I cannot imagine how I found the time to write music. I seldom did fewer than four shows a week with the orchestra, and then there were tours of the northern cities, seaside nights, and all the expeditions to Europe. Yet during this busy time I somehow managed to write my Harmonica Concerto which Tommy Reilly played in London, Warsaw and Hamburg. It was later recorded by the Academy of St Martin-in-the-Fields, conducted by Neville Marriner with Tommy Reilly as soloist. The suite 'From our Village' was commissioned by the BBC and I wrote an oboe concerto for Evelyn Rothwell, which was first played with the Concert Orchestra, and later conducted by Sir John Barbirolli in America. I also wrote a scherzo for orchestra called 'Soho', music expressing the polyglot character of that district. The Oxford University Press asked me to revise and edit some scores for William Walton and when Alan Frank, the music editor, submitted my suggestions to Sir William, he is reputed to have said, 'I trust him, let him get on with it, as long as I don't have to do it'. It was around this time that the English Opera Group entrusted me with performances of Walton's *Façade* (which was entitled 'an entertainment with poems by Edith Sitwell'). I did it on several occasions and with various artists, but the most memorable was at York Festival, in July 1954, with Peter Pears and Edith Sitwell, reciting from her wheel chair.

For some years before I became its conductor, a favourite programme of the Concert Orchestra had been 'Friday Night is Music Night'. Now one of Frank Wade's producers had the idea that a few weeks in the summer should be devoted to 'Friday Night is Seaside Night'. Each week the orchestra would visit a South Coast town, and familiarise holiday audiences with the orchestra they were accustomed to hearing at home. Frank took up this idea with his usual enthusiasm and thoroughness, and for many years these programmes were very popular entertainment. A great feature of every visit was the appearance of that great singer, and personal friend of mine, Owen Brannigan. He tackled everything from operatic arias to Geordie ballads, the latter accompanied by the irrepressible Ernest Lush. The music we played ranged from Mozart to excerpts from *My Fair Lady*, and we usually had a well-known soprano who sang both popular and classical music.

These seaside nights came to have a special family atmosphere on both sides of the house. We visited Eastbourne, Brighton, Folkestone, Margate and other South Coast resorts. It was a day's outing by the sea for the orchestra and many of them brought their families. The car park was like a crèche with odd-looking motor vehicles, caravans and motorbikes, and the air was loud with children playing and babies crying. The orchestra took these expeditions as a happy family joke and of course this atmosphere reached out and embraced the audience who were also in holiday mood and interested to see the people who played for them week by week on the air.

A year after I joined the Concert Orchestra you will understand that I was very proud when the Musician's Benevolent Fund chose our orchestra for the annual St Cecilia's Day concert. An item which won particular praise in the programme was Eric Coates' 'The Three Elizabeths'. The beautiful middle movement, 'Elizabeth of Glamis', is one of the best things he ever wrote, and I often use it to represent British music abroad. In 1958 we were allotted a concert in the Proms at the Albert Hall, where Jean Harvey, an artist who played both violin and piano, played Bruch's Violin Concerto in the first half, and Litolff's Scherzo for Piano and Orchestra in the second half. Joan Hammond sang the Letter Scene from *Eugen Onegin*.

In 1959 Frank Wade arranged a tour of Holland for the orchestra, lasting a week, with visits to the Hague, Amsterdam, Utrecht and Nijmegen. In the Hague we had a tremendous reception, and after the concert the British Ambassador and his wife, Sir Roger and Lady Mason, gave a wonderful supper-party at the embassy for everyone on the tour. We also played at the coronation of the 'Queen of Flowers' in the famous Keukenhof Gardens which were a sea of tulips. In Utrecht we were entertained by the mayor at the historic town hall, and for many of us memories of World War II were revived when we visited Nijmegen.

By 1961 we were earning criticisms like this, following a concert at the Colston Hall, Bristol:

Incredible Concert Orchestra

This is an incredible orchestra. It is a symphony orchestra with the cobwebs blown out, and a theatre orchestra polished to a hard brilliance. And it produces the 'tightest' playing I have ever heard. Attack, vitality, complete unanimity and micro-second accuracy—these are the hallmarks.

How is it done? Partly, of course, by the choice of music. This orchestra does not play dreamy stuff to go with shaded lights. It attacks all the time, piling orchestral effects one on top of the other, biting out the rhythm, drawing every lilt from its melodies. Not one moment's relaxation for orchestra or audience.

But this is not the whole story. Behind yesterday's slick, assured performance lies a stern discipline and unrelenting rehearsal. Vilem Tausky uses every trick in the bag. He makes the most of tonal contrast in every section, he uses his percussion department to the full, and conducts with a fury of concentration that communicates itself to the players.

Versatility is his strong suit, and he almost exaggerates every effect to make sure that the audience (usually, of course, unseen) feels it. From Vaughan Williams' buzzing Wasps to Malcolm Arnold's heathen Scottish Dances, and then on to a full-blooded Rhapsody in Blue, he never missed a trick.

Of course such criticism delights not only the conductor, but every member of the orchestra too, and indeed he could never get these effects without their backing. Certainly 'stern discipline and unrelenting rehearsal' play a part in it, but they would not be much use unless the conductor had the good will of the orchestra behind him.

Perhaps the height of the Concert Orchestra's achievement

during my day was reached when, in 1965, we were invited to do two concerts at the Edinburgh Festival. The highlights of these concerts were Haydn's 'Maria Theresa' Symphony, Prokofiev's D Major Violin Concerto, played by Wanda Wilkomierska, a Polish artist, and the commissioned première of Symphonic Variations by Malcolm Williamson. The second concert ended with scenes from Gershwin's *Porgy and Bess* sung by those wonderful artists, Inia Te Wiata and Mattiwilda Dobbs. They made an unforgettable impression in this dramatic score, full of originality. Also at the same festival I conducted, for the English Opera Group, *Albert Herring* by Britten at the King's Theatre with Kenneth Bowen, Sylvia Fisher and Anne Pashley in the cast.

One of Frank Wade's inspirations had been to use the Kneller Hall Trumpeters from the Royal Military School of Music to open our festival concerts, and contact with the distinguished administration of this school for commonwealth musicians revived my early interest in brass music. I became very friendly with Lieutenant Colonel Basil Brown, and until his retirement I acted as examiner for his conducting pupils, and as guest conductor at the Wednesday night concerts at Kneller Hall. These outdoor evening concerts, which use about a hundred and fifty musicians from all parts of the Commonwealth, each wearing the uniform of his own unit, have an atmosphere all their own. I am still very interested in music for brass and, time permitting, I hope one day to write a gigantic work for voices and brass, designed for the Albert Hall.

During these years I put in almost as much work with Sadler's Wells as I did with the BBC although, of course, the operatic work came in spurts instead of being spread over each week. I should say that every opera took two to three months of intermittent work for me. I found *Nelson*, which was produced at Sadler's Wells in 1954, a most interesting opera to prepare. The music by Lennox Berkeley was brilliantly operatic, and we had a splendid cast including Victoria Elliott, Anna Pollak, Sheila Rex, Robert Thomas, Arnold Matters and David Ward. The subject should have been a most sympathetic one for English audiences, but the press, who were invited to a final dress rehearsal, seemed unanimously prepared to condemn it, and I am afraid it was an opera which undeservedly 'never got off the ground', in spite of a marvellously touching death scene in the cockpit of the *Victory* which I think stands up to any other highlight of modern opera.

In 1954, I also conducted *Il Trittico* by Puccini. These three one-act operas were produced together to make an evening's entertainment, as Puccini intended they should be. The first, *Il Tabarro*, a blood and thunder story of jealousy, and *Gianni Schicchi*, a cynical little comedy of greed, are both fairly often to be heard singly. But *Suor Angelica* a story of convent life, which is certainly true and possibly stems from Puccini's visits to his sister, who had taken vows, should really be played between them to reach the balance the composer had in mind.

I conducted an opera in 1959 which was put on as a result of a referendum by the audience of Sadler's Wells. It was *Andrea Chénier* by Giordano which had never been done in English before and in this production Peter Glossop made a name for himself in his first starring role.

In between times I also conducted many performances of standard operas.

On 18 February 1959 a longed-for wish came true—the première of Dvořák's *Rusalka*, with Joan Hammond in the title role, Charles Craig as the Prince and Howell Glynne as the Watersprite. As I have told you earlier, I had worked on an outstanding Czech production by Dvořák's own librettist. Our producer at Sadler's Wells was Wendy Toye, who filled the stage with the poetry of movement. Our hopes were high, but the piece was ill-fated. On the first night the opera house filled with fog to such an extent that; it was in doubt as to whether a performance could be held; it *was* held under these depressing circumstances, with the result that our tenor was too ill to go on a couple of nights later for the second performance. The press was lukewarm in its reception of the opera, one well known London critic saying, 'It may be all right for Prague schoolgirls on a Saturday afternoon, but it is not my cup of tea'. Yet later, when the Prague Opera Company brought *Rusalka* to Edinburgh, he found it: 'An enchanting piece full of magic and poetry'. This time no praise was too high.

An interesting story underlies the reason that Joan came to be chosen as Rusalka. Some years before, she was making a recording of operatic arias with me and the Royal Philharmonic Orchestra. One morning the 'Ave Maria' by Max Bruch was scheduled for recording, but the orchestral material did not arrive in time from Germany, so I said to Joan: 'Now is our chance, let's do the 'Moonsong' from *Rusalka*,' a hitherto unknown aria in England. Walter Legge, who was in charge, surprisingly agreed, and the 'B-side' became a best selling record which is still in constant demand. As a result of this record the BBC invited us to do a full broadcast of *Rusalka* with Rowland Jones as the tenor, and it may have been this performance that influenced Norman Tucker to put on the opera at the Wells.

Many years before this I had made records with Joan for HMV and also recordings for Columbia of *Rigoletto* and *The Bartered Bride*, with James Johnston and Howell Glynne. During the time I was a staff conductor with the BBC I made many records with EMI, including *Die Fledermaus*, *The Gipsy Baron*, *The Land of Smiles*, *The Count of Luxembourg*, *The Arcadians* and also a whole series of recordings with Semprini. EMI also made two records featuring me as conductor. There was another occasion where the recording didn't go as planned, and I had a lucky idea. We were supposed to record duets with Joan Hammond and Charles Craig, when Charles was unable to turn up at the last moment, due to throat trouble. The orchestra and technical staff were assembled at a cost to the company of about £4,000. Suddenly I had an idea: 'Why don't we make a record of light operatic French overtures, beginning with Méhul's *Two Blind Men of Toledo*?' We phoned the BBC for the material, and within an hour were making what turned out to be a very successful record.

Sadler's Wells were beginning preparations for a new venture. They wanted to put on light opera in a larger house and launched the idea with a production of *Die Fledermaus* at the Coliseum in 1959. This theatre has now become their permanent home under their title of the English National Opera. Wendy Toye's production of *Die Fledermaus* was lavish, full of new sparkling ideas, one of which was the enactment, through a gauze, during the overture, of the happenings before the curtain rises. This idea came in for some criticism, but I found it a charming inspiration. James Bailey did the décor and dresses, and for the party scenes the huge revolving stage looked like a gigantic wedding cake. Victoria Elliott was Rosalinda, Rowland Jones, Alfred, June Bronhill, Adele and Anna Pollak a memorable Orloffski. It was a very successful production and was followed by *The Land of Smiles* with Charles Craig as Sou-chong and Elizabeth Fretwell as Lisa. Sadly, this was not such a success with the public as *Die Fledermaus*, although Craig delighted his audiences with 'You are my Heart's delight' and Elizabeth Fretwell made an excellent character study of the ambassador's daughter, while Mi was one of June Bronhill's most touching roles.

In 1966 Sadler's Wells mounted an opera which had great personal significance for us, as the composer had dedicated it to Peggy and me, and I conducted it. It was *The Violins of St Jacques* by Malcolm Williamson. I had great faith in this opera which had an excellent story by Patrick Leigh Fermor. It was a truly operatic subject, and I felt Malcolm's music had just the quality and character which it needed. As was the case with *Nelson*, I never felt it had the support of the press and the public that it deserved.

Some conductors, and I am among them, are lucky enough often to have in the audience, watchful eyes and sharp ears—I refer to those of conductors' wives. They grow very discerning about the feel of an audience and report back as to whether attention was concentrated, whether certain passages were too difficult for the audience, and whether this performance was in general more or less satisfactory than others. They also sometimes hear some amusing comments.

This particular story does not concern music, but the theatre. Peggy had been with me to a production of *The Ideal Husband* by Oscar Wilde. As the audience streamed out there was in front of her a well dressed, prosperous-looking quartet. They might have been celebrating a successful business deal. 'Thanks very much, old chap,' said one man,' I haven't laughed so much for a long time'.

'Glad you enjoyed it,' replied the other. 'I think myself Shaw is always so witty'.

On another occasion Peggy was on her way to a matinée of *Hansel and Gretel* at Sadler's Wells when Augustus John leapt onto the bus and sat next to her. Lifting the famous wide-brimmed black hat, he said, 'Good afternoon, madam, I'm on my way to *Hansel and Gretel* at the Wells. Do you think I shall enjoy it?'

'I do hope so,' said Peggy. 'I am going there too'.

Unfortunately her friend gave the show away, by leaning over and saying, 'Do you know you are speaking to the conductor's wife?'

At another performance at Sadler's Wells, the company were taking their bows and, behind Peggy, sat a very knowing lady, who kept her companion informed as to what was going on. 'You see that rather stout man they are clapping. That's Harry Powell-Lloyd the producer, and now that dark tall one, that's Vilem Tausky, the conductor'. But she had got it wrong, and there are at least two people who will go through life thinking that I am Harry and Harry is me.

The last story concerns another knowledgeable lady. This happened at the Arts Theatre in Cambridge. Peggy was expecting guests and so she took her seat early, in the front row of the dress circle. Behind her came two old ladies who settled themselves with much rustling of the programme. One said, 'Vilem Tausky is conducting'.

'Good,' replied the other,' I like him'.

'He usually brings his wife' said the first,' and she sings for him. She isn't here today'.

'What a pity!' said the second.

Peggy still wonders from time to time who they had in mind!

Unfortunately, in my world of the BBC, in 1965 Frank Wade became ill and had to undergo a serious operation. He battled valiantly during convalescence and was able to come back to us for a time in 1966, but it was obvious that he was not strong enough to make a complete recovery and at the same time carry out his responsibilities, so he retired. With his departure and the appointment of his successor, there came many changes and a new role was assigned to the Concert Orchestra. In view of the fact that I was by now doing a great deal of outside work—even having to refuse other interesting propositions—and also that I was not entirely in sympathy with the new plans for the Concert Orchestra, it was mutually decided that I should retire as staff conductor, while continuing to conduct the orchestra from time to time. And so, in 1967, I became a freelance conductor for the second time in my career.

12 Cakes and Ale: freelance by choice

My diary tells me that on Boxing Day 1953 I conducted a matinée of *Hansel and Gretel* at Sadler's Wells and a performance of *Il Trovatore* at Covent Garden the same evening. I suppose that is not most people's idea of how to spend a Christmas holiday! So in case this whole chronicle might give the impression that my days were spent only in travelling, rehearsing and performing, I think it only fair to tell you how and when Peggy and I squeezed in some pleasure and recreation.

It must be remembered that the conductor is an entertainer, and therefore in his job he enjoys a good deal of 'built-in' social life. He enjoys meeting the public, and very often those responsible for his appearances will arrange hospitality for him. I recall so many lovely parties before, after, and sometimes in the interval of concerts, and very often private invitations from those attending the concert. Sometimes the conductor is invited to stay with the officials who organize the concert or festival, sometimes with a personal friend. After first nights at the opera everybody is dying to let off steam and talk about the show and how it went, and the management nearly always give an opportunity for this. We are entertained with every degree of refreshment, from tea served in a jug to champagne and smoked salmon—it is the warm hearts, not only the elegance of the refreshment that is appreciated.

At seaside nights we were often guests of the civic corporation for the day, and I remember, during the war, sitting next to a Lord Mayor at lunch when he asked me about the Czech Navy. Like Shakespeare he thought that there is a seaboard to Bohemia.

I looked hard at my plate and murmured something about gunboats on the Danube. It was an embarrassing moment!

When we were first married the only holidays that finance and domestic responsibilities allowed were an occasional two or three days in Manchester for Peggy. It was not the grim holiday it might sound, for she usually came when I was doing some special programme, such as a broadcast of *Dalibor*, or part of the Dvořák symphonic cycle. On another night we might go to a Hallé concert, and there were always two or three theatres to choose from in those days. Anyway, it was a treat to be together without other responsibilities.

By 1952 our financial position had improved enough for us to take our first holiday abroad. We went to a little hotel by the sea in Brittany, having called on my cousin, Theddy, in Paris on the way. Hotel du Centre at Rothéneuf was an enormous success, with wonderful cooking by Madame Jugant, and we bathed, and walked for miles and scrambled over the rocks to our hearts content. It was there that we found that the familiar '*On reçoit avec ses provisions*' had been translated into English on a large wall 'Welcome with baskets'.

By 1955 we had acquired a car, and the next year we drove it to northern Italy, finally landing up at a *pensione*, recommended to us by the Wades, at Celle in Liguria. We found that no one walks in Italy, but we enjoyed having the landscape to ourselves and walking to isolated villages, and for the first time seeing oranges and lemons growing on the trees.

Then we bought our first new car, a Hillman Minx, and in 1957 we drove to the South of France to visit my old wartime haunts, Agde, Pézenas and Béziers. In Pézenas we found the faithful girl who had kept a box of my music all through the hostilities and had sent it to me at her own expense when the war ended. She was now the wife of a garage proprietor and the mother of a daughter of ten. We also went to see Monsieur Pommier, the organist of St Madeleine in Béziers, who had a tribe of children, known in my day as the organ pipes. This beautiful church was used by the Czech Army for their own services and concerts and our military band had played there at the Messe de Noël. Madame Pommier had fed and entertained the Czech musicians like her own children. By 1957, when we arrived there on our sentimental journey, one of the organ pipes, Jean Bernard, had grown up to be a very good pianist. A few years later he won the Prix de Rome and a special prize at the Paris Conservatoire, and he has recently played in the Proms. The Pommiers arranged a party for us at which neighbour after neighbour appeared, each bearing a bottle or a gâteau, and all with some special musical offering to make. I remember the evening ended with Jean Bernard and myself playing 'God save the Queen' in different styles on two pianos.

After this we became island specialists, beginning with Elba. On our first visit Peggy had, in a nightmare, a vivid impression of the spirit of Napoleon still ranging the island in search of freedom. The second year we went our plane was late, and when I saw we would never catch our train connection to the boat I penetrated even to the pilot's cabin, begging him to put on speed. As we arrived at Pisa and the disembarkation officer came out to meet us, I struggled to explain to her in Italian that we had missed our connection. Smiling, she let me struggle, and then said in faultless English, 'Don't worry, Mr Tausky, we have a taxi ready for you. There is no charge; it is the least we can do when we enjoy your broadcasts so much. I have been listening to you while you were in the air'. So we were conveyed, at breakneck speed, a hundred kilometres to Piombino where we just caught the last boat to Elba.

We went twice to Sardinia where we travelled beyond the ordinary range of visitors, attending a Sardinian village wedding, where everyone, including ourselves, gathered around the nuptial bed (without occupants), drinking liqueurs, one after the other, coloured like traffic lights, to the health of the bride and groom. Peggy ended the wedding by being hoisted by strong Sardinian hands on to the back of a donkey.

We were present, too, at a gathering of four thousand Sardinians in national dress, many of them mounted on horseback. We also celebrated the Feast of the Redeemer by climbing with the pilgrims to a mountain top where we ate roast sucking pig, grilled on charcoal.

In 1960 we acquired our great and lasting treasure, our beloved Rose Cottage which is our defence and solace against the changes and chances of this mortal life. For many years we had visited old family friends who lived in a little Oxfordshire village near Thame. When our thoughts turned to the possibility of a retreat for ourselves, we always thought of Towersey, an unspoilt village, an hour's run from London, with one shop and a little grey church. Eventually an opportunity occurred to buy a small cottage, 'two up and two down', half of it built in 1749, and the rest very discreetly modernized some five years before our purchase. It has a long cottage garden in front and windows on both sides of the main rooms. In front we look on to the garden, and at the back on to fields, where there may be cows, horses, pigs, even sheep sometimes, according to Farmer Smith's needs of the moment. He rents the field and lives a few doors away.

This cottage has been a pleasure not only to us, but to our children and grandchildren, who use it for holidays when we are away, and to friends who we think are in need of a rest and change. We also have a long string of visitors who love to come for the day, and go back in the evening with flowers from the garden and half a dozen eggs from the farm.

When we first arrived our next door neighbour was a real countryman who had lived all his life in Towersey. Owing to the exigencies of the 1914 war, he had never learned to read or write. This proved no disadvantage to him as he had worked on the railways, helped to run a coal business, could turn his hand to any job on a farm, and was the village authority on the boundaries of everyone's land.

In our early days the village children, who go to school in Thame by bus, had little to do with themselves in the winter evenings after 4 o'clock, so Peggy wrote a little play for them to act at Christmas time; it was a great success. Towersey already had its own summer village festival established, and I started to arrange an annual concert for this. Gradually it became the custom for the children to perform a nativity play at Christmas and an item in the village festival concert in the summer. This was great fun, but hard work too. I asked professional friends to perform for us, and so we had Rowland Jones, Elizabeth Simon, Madge Stephens and Jean Curphy, as well as gold medallists—pianists and violinists—from the Guildhall School.

I think our outstanding performance was in July 1966 when we did the entry and exit of the animals from *Noye's Fludde* by Britten. Peggy had fifty children from four villages to cope with at rehearsals, but our great triumph was that Owen Brannigan came and sang Noah for us. He was wonderfully impressive in our little church, and he took great trouble with the children beforehand. Not only did he give us his services, but he left his own costume (worth £200) for the use of the schoolmaster who was singing Noah on the Sunday. Owen felt this part very deeply, and he specially asked that no one in the audience should speak to him as he left the church. We arranged that he should step straight into a car and be driven the few hundred metres to our cottage. Unfortunately we all forgot that he would need a key to get in. Our neighbour had quite a shock when a dignified, bearded figure in flowing robes, staff in hand, rapped on his door and asked him to open our cottage for him. Owen took all this as a great joke, and later went to chat with everyone in the village hall.

Of course Towersey has changed with the years, and is not quite the dreamy little village it once was. Many new houses and bungalows have been built and the village has now a social life of its own, but in the eighteen years we have lived there the outlook from our windows is unchanged, as are the one shop, the pub and the church.

To enjoy the pleasure of Rose Cottage I still need to work to earn the money to pay for it. In 1964 the Opera School gave their final brilliant performance of *Fra Diavolo* by Auber, to which I invited Gordon Thorne who had been head of music in the BBC in Manchester, and was then principal of the Guildhall School of Music. Evidently he liked the performance, for he asked me to prepare *The Merry Wives of Windsor* with his opera students. The following year I conducted the end-of-year performance of Wolf-Ferrari's *School for Fathers*. Unfortunately after this performance Gordon became seriously ill, and died the following spring. His successor was Allen Percival who asked me in 1966, after my retirement from the Concert Orchestra, to become senior tutor to the opera students, and later I became director of opera, a post which I still hold. Indeed, handing on my knowledge after so many years of work in the opera house is one of my most rewarding occupations. Dennis Maunder is our very experienced producer and, together with the principal, we hold auditions designed to find the best voices, and hold in proportion the various male and female voices which will be suitable to our class work and productions.

We try to give the students a course which covers as wide a range of opera as possible, and the choice of opera studied each term has to be considered in the light of the voices available. We choose repertoire operas, and sometimes seldom-produced operas. It is also important to give students the opportunity to study operas of different periods. We have commissioned contemporary operas by Geoffrey Bush and Peter Wishart, and, more recently, Carey Blyton and Patric Standford. We give three weeks of public performances a year in London, and one of the most important events is a professional week in the early summer at the Arts Theatre, Cambridge. Students and staff enjoy this week thoroughly, and it is followed by a week's performances of the same opera in our own theatre in the Barbican School.

In 1973 Allen Percival asked me to take over the course for advanced conductors. We have applications from quite a number of different countries, but we can accept only three or four students for this course. They study both symphonic and operatic music, and use the Guildhall orchestra for their practical experience. Each student takes his turn at being my assistant in preparing the end of term opera, then he has the opportunity to conduct a performance. In technical matters I try to teach them through the same traditional rules which I learned myself, but in matters of interpretation I leave them as free as possible to carry out their own ideas, yet always in relation to the intention of the composer. I dissuade them as far as possible from thinking in terms of 'my Mozart' or 'my Beethoven', or other similar egotistical attitudes. I always advise them not to waste much time in talking to the orchestra about why they want certain effects, but simply to carry out their own ideas through technical directions. It is my experience that nothing bores an orchestra more than long explanations from the conductor as to the reasons for his interpretations.

Now that I am freelance I am able to expand the contacts I have formed with major English orchestras, and I can accept invitations from the City of Birmingham Symphony Orchestra, the Royal Liverpool Philharmonic, the Hallé, the Royal Philharmonic, the Philharmonia, and the London Symphony Orchestra.

I have also renewed the flirtation with music for brass which has interested me since childhood. My connection with the Royal Military School of Music stimulated this interest as did BBC producer Geoffrey Brand who in early days had played the trumpet for me in the Covent Garden Orchestra. He made brass music his special interest in the BBC and eventually left them to become editor of *The Bandsman* and conductor of the National Youth Brass Band. Through his influence I conducted and adjudicated at the National Brass Band competitions at the Albert Hall, an experience I enjoyed so much that in 1972 I wrote the test piece 'Concert Overture' for the competition. For the BBC I also acted as adjudicator, together with Harry Mortimer and Eric Ball, for the exciting weekly national competition *Challenging Brass*.

In 1969 came a late blossoming of those early childhood days when I listened to Viennese music in the park, for suddenly I found myself an authority on it. This was no seeking of my own, but nowadays many of the invitations I receive are to conduct concerts of Viennese music. I really am at a loss to know exactly how this came about, but I imagine that in the days of the Concert Orchestra we played many waltzes and marches by Viennese composers, together with works by Mozart, Haydn and Schubert in a lighter vein, and that Victor Hochhauser, the impresario, must have listened to some of these, because he wrote and offered me a concert of Viennese music at the Albert Hall. Since then, each winter, I have done a series of concerts which fill the house on a Sunday night with over six thousand people. I have only one grumble, and that is that Mr Hochhauser doesn't believe that I know other Viennese pieces which people would enjoy. He likes the same programme time after time, and I sometimes wonder where the audience comes from. As a result of these concerts, orchestras in different parts of the country want similar programmes and now I have become type-cast as a specialist on Viennese music.

During this freelance period the BBC has given me the opportunity to give several talks on Czech musicians, including Martinů, Janáček, Dvořák and Smetana, as well as Weinberger and Leo Fall. I have also done complete operatic broadcasts of *Dalibor* by Smetana, *Schwanda the Bagpiper* by Weinberger, *The Kiss* by Smetana, *Jenufa* by Janáček and the first performance in Britain of his opera *Osud* (Fate). In this last opera the chief part was sung magnificently by Marie Collier. In fact it was the last work she was ever to sing, and the circumstances held an almost unbelievable coincidence.

In the opera the heroine falls to her death from the balcony during a struggle with her mother. After the recording, which took place at the Camden Theatre, Martin Penny, who had coached the opera, met Marie on the stairs, and said to her, 'Come on Marie, the party is on the top floor.'

She gave him a strange look and, quoting from the opera, said, 'Their voice shall be heard no more'.

Before the recording of her beautiful voice was broadcast, Marie was dead, having fallen accidentally and tragically from the window of her flat.

In 1973 I was made a member of the BBC Music Advisory Council. I understand that the reason for this was my many years of practical experience in broadcasting music of all kinds.

An invitation reached me in 1974 to return to Czechoslovakia to conduct opera and broadcast symphony concerts. I hope my story has convinced you that I have enjoyed very much making a place for myself as a musician in Britain, and you will also understand it was of the greatest satisfaction to me to be called back to perform again in the country of my first part setting.

13 The return of the native

This invitation amounted to a State invitation, as all visiting artists are engaged by the State.

It so happened that the visit lay for the most part in Brno and Olomouc, the towns in which I had received my musical education. From Olomouc it was easy to visit Přerov where the first seventeen years of my life had been spent.

After an absence of thirty-six years I returned to Czechoslovakia in October 1974. It was not such an emotional occasion as one might expect, for eight of the nearest members of my family had vanished in 1945, and when communications were opened again, despite all efforts to trace them, they were among those who were never heard of again. My only near relative left is my brother who, after some hard times, had succeeded in establishing himself and his family in Canada where I was delighted to visit him in 1973, and again in 1977.

For this reason my return was not a very dramatic occasion and I think Peggy, who accompanied me, was slightly disappointed that when we stepped from the aeroplane I did not, as Chopin did, lift a handful of soil to my lips, nor sleep with some under my pillow, as was his wont on his travels in exile.

Although I had no reunion with my immediate family, I was looking forward to contacting some old friends, both professional and personal. In this I was more fortunate.

There are people who believe that no circumstance is an accident; that every happening has both sequence and purpose; that life is a jig-saw in which one day we shall see how the pieces fit. Whether that is so or not, I find it strange beyond words that this should occur just as we were writing this book. It also happens that the visit to Czechoslovakia was none of my seeking. The negotiations, in which I was determined to take no active part, lasted for over a year—but eventually I arrived in Czechoslovakia.

Of course the years I spent there came back to me so vividly as I looked at the houses where I lived, the cafés where, as young men, we met to write our operettas and the academies where those great teachers, most of them now dead, disciplined our unruly musical ideas.

I went first to Brno, where I was due to take a rehearsal of Smetana's opera *The Secret*, which I was to conduct the following week. Of course I was delighted to find a trumpet and a double bass player who had been in the orchestra when I last conducted it, and two members of the chorus who remembered me. When I returned after my opera engagement in Ostrava I had more time to pursue my old contacts.

The director of the Janáček Academy, Buriánek, asked me to see him. He remembered, at the age of fourteen, hearing me conduct Mendelssohn's *Midsummer Night's Dream* in a full performance produced by Kvapil, Dvořák's librettist. We had a wonderful chat, and among the people I met there was the professor of horn at the Academy — Šolc. It transpired that he was the son of the conductor of those Sunday concerts in the park. I told him how his father gave me my first chance to conduct in public at the age of ten.

We went to Ostrava by train, and it was thrilling to see the countryside through which I had travelled on most weekends so many years ago. Apart from far too many pylons in the country outside Brno, I was surprised how little it had changed. Fields of golden stubble shone in the October sun, mountains of sugar beet lay awaiting transport, and toy churches with bulbous spires marked each village where red-cheeked apples hung in every garden.

I was coming to Ostrava to conduct Beethoven's *Fidelio*. It was a typical performance of Continental opera, as it had been years ago. Leonora was a soprano from the Budapest Opera House, who could not speak a word of Czech. She sang the part in Hungarian. The dialogue was adjusted so that other people outlined the argument of her speeches and she had only to make the simplest responses, such as yes or no. It reminded me of the first opera I conducted—Puccini's *Turandot* with Zinka Milanov singing in Croatian, Jan Kiepura in Italian and the rest of the cast in Czech. On arrival we were shown to a beautiful suite of rooms in the Palace Hotel immediately facing the theatre, and invited to attend a performance for children of Smetana's *Hubička* (The Kiss) at 10 o'clock on Sunday morning.

The theatre itself is rather a surprise, for it is an old building which was bombed back and front during the war. The outer shell has been restored in a quite acceptable compromise of architecture, but inside money and taste have made it a charming gold and white auditorium in the rococo style, a warm and graceful welcome to the audience.

The children came on foot with their teachers, and in buses from outlying districts and villages. They were all dressed as for a special occasion. The girls had pretty party dresses and bright hair-ribbons, the boys carefully brushed hair and special suits. All their faces shone with expectancy. No whistling or shouting, no bubble gum, no feet on the backs of seats! A fatherly director of education addressed them before the curtain went up. The introduction he gave them was a new way of looking at Smetana's operas, even for me. He told them that in the four great folk operas Smetana illustrated four different aspects of peasant life. In *The Bartered Bride* he pictured life in a Czech village, in *The Two Widows* he showed life on a farm, in *The Kiss* he was illustrating the Czech temperament, while in *The Secret* he described life on the frontiers of Sudetenland. Both the latter operas show the typical Czech tendency to obstinacy over small matters—hardheadedness we call it. It was a first rate performance and no trouble was spared. The production was charming and every singer gave of his best. When we went backstage afterwards the principals all had dressers and wig-mistresses. It was a full-scale performance especially for the children. We congratulated the director, and he laughed and said, 'We think it is better for them than listening non-stop to pop music!' All rather different from my earliest days of lurking between the double basses in an extemporized concert hall.

Before I go on with my own story, I must tell you how impressed I was with a bundle of programmes sent to me by the secretary, with a polite note saying, 'I hope these may tempt you to visit us again.' The programme for *Jenufa* had a challenging portrait of Janáček on a black, white and grey cover. Inside were two pages of facsimile script with his musical notes superimposed, and two pages devoted to his own account of his difficulties in getting his opera accepted. There was a delightful programme for *The Two Widows* in palest yellow and white tapestry paper, with witty little drawings of Czech folklife in the margins and an old photograph of Smetana with a reproduced newspaper article about him by Janáček. The programme for *Jacobin* by Dvořák was in brown with beautiful drawings in sepia illustrating Czech life of this period and a fascimile letter by Dvořák about the opera.

Each programme was an admirable preparation for the audience, a perfect illustration of the atmosphere and character of the opera. When I mentioned this to the director he said mildly, 'I never really thought about it like that, in each case I just asked someone I thought would do it well'.

British people would find the town of Ostrava, which could be compared to a big English industrial town, in some aspects depressing and drab. The buildings are dark grey and no attempt has been made to beautify or mitigate the conditions under which the people pursue their daily lives. They themselves are dressed in clothes suited to the work they do, but, like the children, they are transformed when you see them at the theatre in the evening. You would never guess that fifty metres behind this elegant little theatre lies a coalmine and that from the window of my rehearsal room I could see the coal lift at work. Yet these are the people from whom the poetic lyricism of *Rusalka*, the musically revolutionary character of *The Little Vixen* and the ironic humour of Karel Čapek sprang. Under the utilitarian exterior they are still people who respond to poetry, music and art.

I was very much reminded of the industrial areas of Wales,

where the population is employed in steelworks or mines and the whole surroundings of their daily life are unaesthetic to a degree. But if you talk to any Welshman about music, his native country, or any subject that touches on his emotions, you will find the poet beneath.

In Czechoslovakia it was clear that the State was ready to expend enthusiasm and money on keeping alive the tradition of Czech culture. It would seem that they feel this to be of more importance than the quality of goods used in everyday life. Material circumstances can be improved at any time, but a generation without culture is a lost generation, according to their point of view.

I had set aside Sunday for a pilgrimage to Přerov, where I spent the first seventeen years of my life, but the Přerov of my childhood has vanished and this, perhaps, was the saddest moment of my visit to Czechoslovakia.

Our house still stands, solid and with a certain dignity. We found it locked and empty. The police own it and I understand that on weekdays visas and permits are issued from it, but no-one lives there. It is dirty and crumbling. The square of seventeenth-century houses has been replaced by modern flats, and the thirteenth-century castle has been painted yellow. The elegant little restaurant which served the theatre and concert hall has been turned into an ordinary café. But we found another restaurant to lunch in, opposite the station, where we were waited on by a beautiful young Jewess of about seventeen. I asked her if there were many Jewish families in the town. 'Only ourselves and one other family,' she said, 'and the nearest synagogue is in Olomouc.' In my day there were about a hundred Jewish families in Přerov.

There was one fortuitous meeting. Just as we walked from the station a lady came running after us. 'Surely it is Mr Tausky? . . . I am Rudolf Firkušný's sister.'

Ruda and I were two of three students who worked with Suk at the Meisterschule in Prague. Maria had not expected to see me in Přerov, but had booked a seat for my opera in Olomouc. She wanted to tell me that, on the evening before my father was transported from Přerov to an unknown destination, he came to see her. She was probably the last person to speak to him and he asked her to thank Ruda for letting him know that I was alive and in France. She constantly repeated the number of the house where I could get the key of the cemetery if I wanted to visit my mother's grave. I did not go: my mother lives in my heart and in her children and grandchildren. For us Přerov is only a dot on the map, the place where we were once young and happy together is gone for ever.

Next came my visit to Olomouc where I conducted Puccini's *Madame Butterfly*, while Konvalinka, the resident director of opera, went to Prague. I must say that of my triangle of towns this is the least spoilt. We were therefor three days and I felt very happy. Olomouc is the seat of an archbishop, and I am glad to say that they have left him some of his dignity. We arrived on a golden October day and once again the theatre had arranged a delightful suite of rooms for us in one of the old-established hotels.

Our first visit was to the grey Gothic cathedral, where the Austrian Empress, Maria Theresa was crowned. It is magnificent and overwhelming, but we fell in love with the surrounding buildings with their Baroque rounded mouldings which softened to a butter-yellow in the last rays of the sun. They fulfilled the same function as the houses in an English cathedral close, and the cobblestoned yards and green lawns gave the same air of timeless repose.

Olomouc had always been a very special city for me. Most people who follow any particular profession find that there is one period in their apprenticeship when the core of the knowledge they are going to use for the rest of their life is established. Interest may begin before this formative period, specialisation and experience must be added to it afterwards, but it is usually during one particular time that the foundation of knowledge is laid. For me, I feel this was the years at Olomouc between the ages of eleven and seventeen.

While I was enjoying conducting *Madame Butterfly*, Peggy was having rather a trying time in the director's box with his wife. We had been slightly dismayed on hearing of this arrangement, because we knew that Madame Konvalinková had not a word of

English. However we quite thought someone who spoke English would be asked to make up the party. It was not so! The first act was not too bad, each was able to convey to the other by smiles and gestures their appreciation of the performance.

At the end of the first act Paní Konvalinková managed, 'See Maestro?'. And Peggy, who never comes round in the interval, clutched gladly at this straw. Unfortunately, on their return to the box, which had a step in it and was abominably lit, she fell flat on her face, which didn't help. The second act passed in silence, but at the end Madame turned with a beaming smile and announced in broken accents, 'It's a long, long way to Tipperary'. Her final sally as the curtain fell on the third act was, 'Thumbs up!'

I had never conducted in Olomouc before, but I cannot tell you how many times I did so, in my imagination, between the ages of eight and ten. At home we had an album of overtures for the piano. Just inside the cover was an inspiring picture of an opera house, all red and plush, with a brass orchestral rail, boxes all around, the conductor in position with baton raised, the red curtains closed, and an atmosphere of keenest anticipation. This picture inflamed my imagination and, whenever I could get the music room to myself, I chose an operatic score, placed beside it the picture of the opera house, and bowing low to the imaginary audience, began my performance of *Faust* or *Carmen*. Needless to say, the opera never reached a conclusion, but after I had performed as much as I could comfortably manage, with another deep bow I finished with the words, 'You have just heard a performance of . . .'

I never chose Mozart operas. I had the sense to know I couldn't keep the tempo going! I am glad to tell you that when, half a century later, I actually *did* conduct in Olomouc, it was a rewarding occasion and a full house. We had a Butterfly with a beautiful voice and, although it was only her second performance, she gave a sensitive and thoughtful performance of the role. I think it is more than likely that we shall hear more of this young Czech singer, Eva Kinclova. Since I was there, she has already been heard in Prague.

After the performance, one of the members of the orchestra brought me a picture of a local amateur choir in Přerov with his father in it. The very choir who had sung in my Revue, written when I was fifteen.

On my return to Brno it so happened that our hotel lay not three minutes away from Smetana Street, the site of the old Janáček Conservatoire. So this was one of my first expeditions, and over forty years melted away as if they had never been. For Smetana Street was less changed than anywhere else in Brno. It was still a wide, tree-lined avenue. Janáček's house had changed least of all and the Conservatoire, which he had founded from an original organ school in 1882, with nine pupils and three teachers, was still there too. In 1918, when the new republic was established, it had become a State Conservatoire with one hundred and eighty-six pupils, thirteen teachers and its own buildings.

In September 1927 I was just seventeen, and I felt very shy and self-conscious as, for the first time, I walked up Smetana Street, past the house of the great man himself, which lay on the left-hand side of the forecourt, to begin my career at the Janáček Conservatoire. Each of the two hundred pupils felt both humble and grateful for we all knew that we owed our chance of becoming musicians to the devoted efforts of one man. Since then a new Janáček Conservatoire has been built in Brno, and the Smetana Street building is now the Janáček Museum, with his house and garden kept as nearly as possible as they were in his day. The curator, a charming young lady who is an authority on Janáček, opened the house for us. She laughed when I said accusingly, 'You have moved his hand-painted Slovakian chest, it used to stand between the two windows'.

'The central heating was bad for it,' she said. Otherwise all the dear familiar things were there, even Pani Janáček's mending-basket. I asked if it were possible to see the last few pages of his score of The House of The Dead. I wanted to look again at the ending in which I had been involved for the posthumous performances in 1930. My doubts were still real after 44 years! The modern feeling is that Janáček saw far into the future; indeed did he not prove something of a prophet? His final thought was of the remaining captives, whom he saw as a symbol of suffering humanity. She agrees with the original ending and, on a necessarily superficial perusal of the score, so did I. I told her of an English version of one of Janáček's feuilletons called *The Three Hens* which I translated recently for our Guildhall School magazine. I sent them a copy for inclusion in the archives. I was asked to sign the book of memory and left, feeling that the spirit of this man was so great that it lives on, even in a physical sense, in this place where he worked so ceaselessly both for people and for music.

The visit to Janáček's house brought back vivid memories of the great teachers who were responsible for transmitting his new ideas to the musical world. I was lucky enough to be taught by them. It was sad to think that all these splendid musicians were dead, but a journalist to whom I spoke said, 'You know your old principal, Jan Kunc, is still alive. He is ninety-one and a half, would you like to see him? I could bring him to the radio station when you make your recording.'

So that dear old man came along with his nurse companion, giving up his midday snooze to be with me. He seemed to remember me, and we embraced with fervour. I was rehearsing a modern piece by Schurmann. He was keen to listen, so I gave him a score. It apparently annoyed him that he had to put on glasses, but to my surprise he followed attentively for a couple of hours. At the end he said to me, 'It is wonderful how purposefully you rehearse, achieving such light and shade, and getting so much detail into focus,' to which I replied, 'And who taught me, and where did I learn it?'

He departed, chuckling happily. For me this was one of the highlights of my visit.

The press and photographers in Brno were most friendly, and were intrigued to find out how it felt to be back in Czechoslovakia, conducting an orchestra, after an absence of thirty-six years. We felt they had to be very discreet in everything submitted to print. Peggy wrote an article in English about Czech music that I had promoted in England, and that was fine, but when she mentioned casually that I had arrived in England penniless and without a coat on my back, the journalist said, 'We'll cut that, they might think it was a reflection on the government of the time'.

One of the photographers, who took some very good shots of me, brought the proofs to a little party held at the evening, and said proudly, 'I have written in English what I feel about your conducting'. This is what he had written: 'This old mug, hearing music of heaven, is bringing with his stick.'

Peggy told him gently, 'It can't be "mug", this is something quite different in English.'

'No,' he said, 'I am sure. I found it in the dictionary.'

We all put our heads together and it transpired that he had wanted to write: 'This old magician hears heavenly music, and brings it to us with a wave of his wand.'

Before I embarked on this visit to Czechoslovakia I made up my mind that I would neither enter into nor engage in political discussions and, rather to my surprise, I found this easy to do. The Czechs seemed in some curious way to understand and accept, without explanation, that politics were taboo for me.

I found much to praise in the people I met. They were as enthusiastic about the arts, as generous and hospitable as they had been in old times. This they showed by filling our room with flowers wherever we went, by charming little souvenirs to take home, and by a series of public and private parties.

To give only two examples. When I arrived at the opera house at Brno there was a parcel for me which, on opening, held a locked box. I had left it with my girlfriend thirty-six years ago. She returned it to the theatre without enclosing an address 'lest it should cause embarrassment'. The box contained only snap-shots and a leather wallet. Luckily I found out her address from other friends and I was able to meet her and thank her personally.

Another delightful surprise was the appearance of three princi-pals, singers who had worked with me in pre-war days. They appeared in my dressing room at the opera house after the performance, each with a little gift, a souvenir of the old days.

I enjoyed conducting *The Secret* in the new opera house—the one where I worked formerly has been converted for straight plays.

The new Janáček Opera House has an enormous stage on which it is difficult to create the intimate village atmosphere essential to *The Secret*. The orchestra and the singing were good, but the production was a little too glossy for my taste. Some months earlier I had done the first performance of this opera in England, at the Camden Festival. The small stage was overcrowded and the production achieved on a shoestring, but in some ways it had a more authentic atmosphere.

In the following year I was invited to Czechoslovakia again, this time to conduct concerts as part of the Slovakian Spring Festival. It was a very interesting tour for me, because I only knew Slovakia as the background of some wonderful holidays. It was rather as if you offered a conductor, resident in Birmingham, three concerts in the Scottish Highlands.

My first concert was at Košice, the capital of East Slovakia. My arrival at Košice got off to a bad start. When I went to unpack I found that, although it was an identical case to mine, the one I arrived with belonged to a civil engineer travelling to Prague. He must have been equally surprised, on opening my case, to find batons and scores. Luckily the director of the orchestra had a friend at the airport who set the wheels turning and, after a slight detour via Amsterdam, my case arrived the next evening.

The city of Košice had considerably increased in size and importance since my time. It had always had a large Jewish population, being on the borders of Hungary and the Ukraine, but, as a result of Hitler's regime, the Jewish element has almost disappeared. The old synagogue has been converted into a fine concert hall. Košice, with a population of about 200,000, has its own State Philharmonic Orchestra and theatre.

This State Orchestra caters for the surrounding districts, and the other two concerts I conducted, with the same orchestra, were at Mischalovce and Humenné. The latter is interesting because there Haydn worked for some time under the patronage of Esterházy. The great hall of this beautiful rococo palace is still used as a concert hall for chamber music and recitals. The rest of the palace has been converted into a newly established conservatoire. Our symphony concert was held in the fine new art centre, opposite the palace.

The Slovaks have always been rather inclined to an inferiority complex concerning the Czechs with their more sophisticated approach to the arts. During the war they were a separate state and since rejoining Czechoslovakia after the war they have developed greatly, both in industry and the arts.

I was able to introduce some contemporary British music into my programmes, which was much appreciated. Among the composers represented were Malcolm Williamson and Gerard Schurmann.

Originally it was planned that I should also conduct an opera in Prague, but it meant waiting in Prague another ten days, and my British commitments did not allow this. These two visits to the country of my birth have done much to heal the wounds of the war. I have been accepted after my long absence, both for my music and for myself. I have been greeted by many old friends as if I had never been away. It has been a very happy return of the native. But England is my home.

Epilogue

So Vilem is going to let me have the last word, as he let me have the first. Very decent of him, I must say. But on second thoughts I deserve it, for he has been a hard taskmaster.

'You haven't said anything about Suk as my teacher.'

'Unless you explain about our next door neighbour, people won't understand what Towersey was like when first we came here.'

'What about my years of association with Semprini?'

'You never told how Vroons and Brouwenstijn were an hour late for the broadcast because they forgot to alter their watches.'

'You say I was disappointed with the reception of *Nelson*, but don't forget that, at the first night party at the Savoy, Vicki was clapped all the way up the River Room.'

And always, always he thinks of these things when I have just finished the place where they would naturally fit in. I find it very difficult to go back, but mostly I do, because I know there will be no peace until he has his way.

For his sixtieth birthday I planned a secret party, a Sunday lunch party, and I tried to get people to represent as many aspects of his life as possible. Bernard Grun, who knew his parents, was there; his niece, Lisa, was over from America; I had people to represent opera, the BBC, and all the different sides of his music making. He himself knew nothing about it until he walked right into the party, having driven in the early hours of the morning from Nottingham.

For the sides of his life that we couldn't represent at the party Jan, his daughter in law, who is an artist, made him, with great

157

patience and skill, a book which was a record of his whole life. His childhood, his teachers, his early triumphs in Czechoslovakia, his soldiering days . . . they were all recorded by means of photos, programmes, posters, letters and Jan's own sketches. There were all the British days too—special operatic occasions, visits abroad for the BBC, happy days at the Guildhall, and many pictures of the family and friends.

Vilem was delighted, and for many days we pored over it, and showed it to all comers. Then, as is the way with such things, it was laid aside and I didn't look at it for perhaps as long as three years. When I saw it afresh, my main impression was what a happy life it showed, and in filling out the story I hope I have made it clear that the man is the music, and the music is the man, the two are inseparable.

It is a life in which many difficulties have been overcome, largely by an infuriating determination to refuse to see that they existed! A life in which service to music has always come first, and yet time has been found for family and friends. A life in which no work has ever been too humble to be done to the very best of his ability, and in which envy and uncharitableness have played no part.

Looking back over the years what can we say but the ancient grace?

'Lord, you have given us so much, grant us one more gift— thankful hearts!'

APPENDIX OF OPERAS AND OPERETTAS

conducted by Vilem Tausky

Albert, E. d'	Tiefland
Arne	Love in a Village
Auber	Fra Diavolo
Beethoven	Fidelio
Berkeley	The Dinner Engagement
	Nelson
Bizet	Carmen
	Djamileh
	Doctor Miracle
	The Pearl Fishers
Blacher	The Flood
	Romeo and Juliet
Blyton	The Girl from Nogami
Boughton	The Immortal Hour
Britten	Albert Herring
	A Midsummer Night's Dream
	The Rape of Lucretia
Bush, G	Lord Arthur Saville's Crime
Chabrier	Une Education manquée
Chailley	Trial by Tea
Cimarosa	Il Maestro di capella
Donizetti	Don Pasquale
	The Night Bell
	Rita
Dvořák	Jacobin
	The Pigheaded Peasant
	Rusalka
Fall	Madame Pompadour
Fibich	S`árka
Flotow	Martha
Giordano	Andrea Chénier
Gluck	L'Ivrogne corrigé
Gounod	Faust
	The Mock Doctor
	Romeo and Juliet
Haydn	La Canterina
Hindemith	The Long Christmas Dinner
Humperdinck	Hansel and Gretel
Kálmàn	Countess Maritza
Léhar	The Land of Smiles
	The Merry Widow
Leoncavallo	Pagliacci
Mozart	Bastien and Bastienne
	Cosi fan tutte
	Don Giovanni
	The Magic Flute
	Marriage of Figaro
	Il Seraglio
Martinů	Comedy on the Bridge
	The Three Marias
Mascagni	L'Amico Fritz
	Cavalleria Rusticana
Massenet	Le Jongleur de Notre Dame
	Le Portrait de Manon
	Werther